The Last American Homestead

The Last American Homestead

Living Life In The Last Frontier

My race in achieving the dream of loving and living life along the Ambler River in the Brooks Range of Alaska and being lucky enough to acquire one of the last Patents through The Homestead Act of Alaska.

DAVID W. MARANVILLE

ISBN: 0999691872
ISBN 13: 9780999691878

TABLE OF CONTENTS

Prologue   vii

1   How It All Began   1
2   Heading North On A Wing And A Prayer   4
3   Alcan 1965   8
4   Welcome To Alaska   17
5   Heading Home   23
6   Return To Alaska On The Blades Of A Helicopter   27
7   Introduction To The Ambler River   36
8   Starting Sunshine Helicopters   53
9   Airplanes And Mary   57
10   Trappers And Dogs   67
11   The Trip Begins   81
12   Here Come The Bears   92
13   Visitors From All Over   100
14   Bringing Out The Airplane.   108
15   The Joy Of Flying   114
16   How Not To Land On A Gravel Bar   119
17   How To Bush-Fix An Airplane   123
18   Gold Panning And Clouds   128
19   Everyday Living In The Wilderness   135
20   Time To Go   147
21   Return To The Cabin   152

PROLOGUE

It was April 17, 1978 and we just loaded the plane with half of the supplies we would need to survive in the wilderness for a minimum of six months. The plane was old, but a completely restored 1943 Howard, one of just 13 left in the world. Don Taylor was the pilot, and a good friend of mine, who had worked with me in the helicopter business a few years before. He had also been the person who restored the plane. When I told him I wanted to fly from Fairbanks into the Brooks Range to build a cabin on a new homestead, he volunteered his services to fly me and a friend, Mary Anderson, and my two kids (Fred was four years old and Michael was two years old), to an airstrip 12 miles from the cabin site. I was just hoping we could catch a ride into the cabin site with Don and he was hoping to land us on a gravel bar close to the cabin once we arrived. To this day I am not sure what we expected because the snow was very deep near the cabin and landing an aircraft would have been a one-time event. As it turned out, the problem of landing at the cabin never presented itself. After loading the aircraft and preparing for takeoff, we crashed.

It was a beautiful spring day in Alaska. The wind was calm and the sky was clear. Michael was up front in Mary's lap and I was in the backseat holding Fred in my lap. Mary was strapped in and I was tied in with a rope on top of the supplies. The supplies were all strapped down to the aircraft floor. To this day, I am not sure why the plane crashed. Maybe the load was too heavy or not balanced correctly. Don may not have been familiar with the flight characteristics of the aircraft because he had not flown it much. The plane had plenty of power with a huge round radial engine on the nose. The tail was huge on the aircraft and possibly responded to the slight crosswind more dramatically than expected. Whatever the cause, as the aircraft rolled down the runway for takeoff, it began to wander back and forth with more extreme movement as the speed increased. Don tried to control the movement with his pedals, but it just got worse. There were aircraft parked on both sides of the runway and soon we realized we would hit one if we didn't get in the air soon. Don pulled back on the controls and the plane started to lift off but swerved hard to the right. On the right side of the strip were several planes and fuel tanks. Just past the edge of the aircraft parking area started the float pond which was still frozen over.

The Howard got off the ground and missed the planes. We might have made it except the aircraft propeller hit a 300-gallon fuel tank on a stand. The plane came down hard onto the frozen float pond breaking the right landing gear off and folding the right wing up after breaking the wing strut. Why the plane never broke through the ice only God knows. We slid to a gentle stop on the ice. I was the only one hurt with a nose bleed from my son's head hitting my nose. The silence was instant, but Don went into action assuring we were all OK. Then without hesitation, he broke out a window since the door on the right side was unusable. We all crawled out and were met by all the people who had come by to see us off. The plane never caught fire and we quickly unloaded all our gear into a pickup truck belonging to Bobby Warren, my son's uncle. Bobby drove the kids over to their grandmother's house where they stayed the night and then he took Mary and me to a friend's house on Chena Hot Spring Road where we proceeded to chug down a bottle of wine and celebrate surviving an airplane crash.

Don's aircraft was never rebuilt and his dream most likely died that day. Mary, the kids and I continued on so the story of The Last American Homestead can be told. I dedicate this book to all the dreamers who have tried and failed only to try again and eventually find their solace in the accomplishment of their dreams.

1

HOW IT ALL BEGAN

I was born and raised in the Pacific Northwest in the state of Oregon. I loved the large trees, mountains, rivers and ocean. My first year in school, the teacher was discussing large mammals found in the Northwest and farther North. I believe we were discussing moose when she mentioned they were found all over North America and Canada. She said many of America's moose were found in Alaska. "Alaska" …just the sound of the word caught my attention. Something inside me sparked and from then on, that spark found a place in my heart and I knew I would go to Alaska. I had to see the mountains and the wildlife. Alaska sounded so big and so free.

Years went by, but eventually I reached the ripe old age of 17. The need to go North had never left my heart. After graduating from high school in 1964, I convinced two of my childhood buddies we needed to go to Alaska. The year was 1965 and I was going to college and working odd jobs. My two buddies, Keith Rohrer and Raymond Reid, helped me find an old car to buy. We bought a 1953 Ford with a flat-head V8 engine -- a college dream car! It was covered with stick-on footprints and racing stripes and we bought it for $23. Of course it needed some work -- the engine smoked so bad that today you would be arrested for the pollution. The front end was worn out and the tires were bald. Only a teenager like me could see the potential. When I suggested to my two buddies we should drive it to Alaska, they thought I was crazy. Each of our dads had different skills which provided different shop tools. Keith's garage contained a machine shop, Ray's garage contained a welding shop and I had the wood working shop with lots of tools. None of us had ever rebuilt a car engine before but what the heck, we were young and not afraid of anything.

During the summer of 1965, we all worked odd jobs and saved our money to finance rebuilding the car and pay for the trip up North. When we told our parents our plans, I know they never believed we would do it. In those days, you could buy a rebuild kit for an engine pretty cheap and it came with all the gaskets, bearings, rings and lots of small parts, but did not come with a new crank or new pistons. After removing the engine and tearing it down, we found a worn out crank and deep grooves in the piston walls. Not to be delayed, we used beer can metal to shim up the crank bearings and cleaned the cylinder walls the best we could. Once again, I don't think our parents believed we would ever get the car to run, or better yet, make it to Alaska.

We planned to leave for Alaska on September 1st. We were still working on the car when that day came and went. We had the engine installed and got it running; it actually ran pretty good.   The engine smoked a little, but we guessed the rings needed seating.   About then, my dad realized I meant what I was saying and was really taking this car to Alaska.   He told me since my birthday was near, he would buy new tires for the car. He gave me his credit card and told me to take it to our local garage and have new tires put on.   Of course, the mechanic at the garage pointed to the worn out front end and said it really needed to be repaired.   I told him to add that to the credit card bill and then I just forgot to give the credit card back to my dad.

By September 3rd, we were packing up the car with all the stuff we would need for the trip.   We had tons of camping gear and $285 saved up between the three of us.   At the last moment, Ray's dad put his foot down and said Ray could not go with us.   I know it broke his heart and it was a sad day for us all.   Still, Keith and I forged ahead and "Alaska or Bust" was painted on the car.   In fact, the whole car had a new paint job.   I remember as we left out of Portland and crossed the bridge into Washington, the engine began to knock.   I looked at Keith and he looked at me and I reached down and turned up the radio.

2

HEADING NORTH ON A WING AND A PRAYER

We realized on our way up to the US/Canadian Border that the engine was going through more oil than anticipated, so we stopped at a K-Mart store and bought a five-gallon jug of re-manufactured oil. The car never let us down during the whole trip. I guess it wanted this Alaska trip as bad as we did.

When we got to the US/Canadian Border, a Customs Agent pulled us over and went through all of our stuff. They then took us inside and checked our identification and asked us how much money we had with us. Proudly we said "$285.00". They said that was not enough money to get to Alaska through Canada and wanted to know if we had any other source of money to make the trip. That's when I remembered my dad's credit card in my wallet. I said "yes, I have a credit card" and I showed him the card. He smiled and said "as soon as you get your tail lights to work, you can go on to Alaska".

The first part of the trip was smooth sailing. Highway 1 was still under construction, but most of it was new pavement. The first day we made it to Hope, British Columbia, Canada which was a fitting start to the long, rough journey ahead to Alaska. Hope is the jump-off point to the Fraser River Canyon. To this day it is one of the most beautiful but dangerous roads in Canada. The road follows the Fraser River to Lytton, then follows the Thompson River to the small town of Ashcroft. Just after Ashcroft comes Cache Creek, then 100 Mile House and then 150 Mile House. When the highway going north was being built, Canada was still using "miles" to determine distance and landmarks, however since then, they have switched to kilometers. The towns had already been named, so over the years they kept the names of 100 Mile House and 150 Mile House and the mileage was from the start of the original highway. Over time, the road has been straightened and the miles have lessened.

Keith and I got off to a late start the next morning and we drove only part of the way through the canyon. The weather was great and the scenery was simply breathtaking. We found a small undeveloped campsite somewhere about the middle of the canyon and we both slept in the car. The old car had bench seats in the front and back so we slept good. Each morning we would drag out the Coleman stove, pots and pans, paper plates and our two spoons, two knives and two forks. We were great at cooking breakfast, but probably a little challenged when it came to cooking dinner. There just weren't any fast food places back then, but we could not have afforded it anyway.

We made it to Prince George, British Columbia the next day. The old car was percolating along just fine as long as we added oil now and again. We kept hoping the piston rings would seat and the oil usage would come to a halt. Eventually the oil usage slowed down, but every time we stopped, we checked the oil.

Fuel in Canada seemed expensive to us. Looking back now, I see what a great deal we were getting. In 1965, Canada was still using the Imperial gallon which was equivalent to approximately 1.2 US liquid gallons. Basically, for every 10 Imperial gallons in Canada we were getting 12 US gallons. Today, fuel in Canada is measured in metric liters and is 3.8 liters to one US gallon of fuel. One dollar per liter works out to US $3.80 which is not a good deal when traveling through Canada and of course one must figure in the exchange rate at any given time.

The map showed two routes we could take to get to the Alaska Highway. In those days, it was referred to as the Alcan (the Alaska-Canadian Highway). One route would take us to the Alcan Highway through Fort St. John, British Columbia and the other route turned off at Chetwynd, British Columbia and went North through Hudson's Hope, British Columbia. The only reason to go to Fort St. John was for the actual start of the Alaska Highway, but we could cut off some miles by going through Hudson's Hope. We decided to take the short cut.

We ended up staying at a pull-off somewhere near Hudson's Hope. There was a lot of activity around Hudson's Hope which was primarily due to the start of the new Bennett Dam project.

I remember the road through Hudson's Hope was all paved and the view of the untamed Peace River was spectacular. The wildlife in the area was plentiful with deer, moose and bears. The road was very steep as we drove out of the Peace River valley and it worked our little Ford flathead engine hard. We had to add oil at the top of the climb. Twenty miles down the road we connected with the Alcan Highway where we found the last gas station before turning left onto the Alcan.

3

ALCAN 1965

The first few miles were paved and we were speeding along at 55 mph enjoying the country. Suddenly the road turned to gravel or rock…whichever you prefer. The road was covered in washboard ripples that shook the poor car and us, half to death. We pulled over to the side of the road and picked up one of the rocks in the middle of the road. Keith held it up in his hand and it was easily the size of a cantaloupe. The sign said "Gravel Road Next 1,275 Miles". Suddenly we knew why we brought two spare tires with us. Fortunately, we never needed them.

The road was so rough in many spots that we had to slow down to 30 miles per hour or slower. Still, the road was drivable all the way to Pink Mountain and then we started driving through construction. We would drive until we got tired and then we would pull over at a wide spot or find a trail going off the main road and camp. Some of the construction areas were so bad with mud, the construction crew would make you wait until one of their big crawler tractors could come back and hook up a cable to your car and pull you through the mud. Fortunately, there was not a lot of traffic.

The majority of vehicles on the Alcan were semi-trucks. When we saw one coming, we got off the road and stopped. If you decided to just meet them head on, and pass on their left, you would lose your windshield. The first time I met a semi-truck coming around a corner, I didn't have time to get off the road. Poor Keith was sound asleep next to me in the front seat. The rock from the oncoming semi-truck was so big that I could see it coming. The rock was about the size of a golf ball and it hit the windshield just left of the rearview mirror. The glass exploded inward covering Keith and the sound was like a gunshot going off. Keith about came out of his skin! The rock did not come through the windshield, but it sure left the biggest fish eye crack I have ever seen on a windshield. After that, we were both very alert to any semi-trucks coming toward us or wanting to pass.

As we motored on up the Alcan, we noticed white crosses at many of the curves. Some curves had dozens of crosses. We soon figured out those crosses were for people who died on that particular curve. A few years later, they stopped putting crosses on the curves. I think the reason was people were trying to count the crosses and they would miss the curve and kill themselves.

In those days, the road was not very straight and the curves on the road were slanted high on the outside and low on the inside which made it fun to drive; you felt like you were driving the Indy 500 races. The road was also very narrow, so trying to see animals coming out of the woods was impossible. Keith and I saw several dead animals along the road and we felt very lucky not to have hit any animals on our trip. Dust was another problem. I could not believe how much dust was on the highway. If a truck passed, it would take several minutes for the dust to settle so you could see where you were going. The dust got into everything. The trunk on the car was not sealed all that good, so everything in the trunk was covered in a fine layer of dust. Inside the cab was not so bad as long as the windows were up. God help you if you lowered a window at the wrong time.

The dust would turn into a slippery slime when wet, which made ice feel like solid pavement. All it took was a little rain and driving became almost impossible. Somewhere along the trip, it got so slippery we decided to pull over and stop for a while. When we got out of the car and slammed the door, the car just slid right off the side of the road and down an eight-foot embankment. We were stunned and unable to do anything to get the car out. We were in the process of emptying everything out of the car to make it lighter when a very nice semi-truck driver came by. He saw our predicament and stopped. He was also having difficulty getting traction on the road, but since he was much heavier than we were, he was able to hook up a chain and pull us out. Consequently, we drove a very short distance that day. When the road would dry out to just a damp surface, the dust would end and the road would get as smooth as a new paved highway and we could drive along at 55 mph without a care in the world.

Once in a while, the engine would start to seize up from lack of oil. We could always tell it needed oil when the engine heat would start to build. When that happened, we would stop, usually near a creek, grab our fishing tackle and march off into the woods following the creek. When we got back to the car, the engine would be cooled down and we could add more oil and move on. The old flathead engine was amazing! Today's engines would just blow up and that would be the end of it.

After about the fifth day, we reached Contact Creek. This was where the two sides, north and south, working on the highway during World War II came together. The highway was just a dirt road that both the Americans and the Canadians worked to complete as fast as possible. They were working from both ends and when they met, it must have been quite a party. Back when Keith and I drove the road, they were working on making it a real highway. Today it is a real highway with wide stretches of straight road and completely paved from one end to the other. The road has been shortened by nearly 200 miles by just straightening out the curves. Keith and I camped at Contact Creek. The weather was sunny and warm, but cool in the evenings. The campground had small standing barrel-type barbecue grills so we cooked the fish for dinner we caught that day and had a great meal. The next morning, we fired up the grill again and cooked the last of our bacon and eggs when the Canadian Robins showed up. These birds are noted as camp robbers for a reason. They are not afraid of anything or anyone. Before we knew it, one of the birds flew down and stole a piece of our bacon. Of course that did not go over well with us so we removed the bacon and heated up the top of the barrel grill to red hot. We then put a small piece of bacon on the grill to see just how daring these birds were. The first couple of birds flew down but when they got close they realized the pan was just too hot. One bird was sitting up on a limb watching the other birds give up. Then he made his move and flew down, landed on the hot grill, walked over and grabbed the bacon and then flew off. His secret was landing on his claws. He had them extended out so only the claws touched the grill. I told Keith those birds were too smart for us.

The next day we continued heading farther and farther North. We camped along the way when we found a campground each evening. Gas stations in those days were spaced about every 100 miles. There were signs telling us how far it was to the next station, but by rule you just didn't pass one up without topping off your tank. Each one of the gas stations was also a lodge and each one was unique. One stop had hats from all over the world nailed all over the lodge ceiling and walls, another had every playboy pin up all over the ceilings and walls and each lodge was well worth going into just to hear the history of what brought them so far out into the wilderness. Today most of those lodges are gone and along with them, a lot of highway history. One other thing most of the lodges had were tow trucks. Some of the wrecked cars and trucks which were parked out back said a lot about how dangerous the road was back then.

We reached Liard River Hot Springs early one morning. I mention it here because today there is a large log cabin lodge, parking area and a fee to go back to the hot springs. When we found Liard River Hot Springs, it was pure luck. We came around a corner and saw an old faded wooden arrow pointing into the woods. All it said was "Hot Springs". The map we had with us showed Liard River Hot Springs somewhere in that area, so we stopped. We followed a trail leading us through a swamp. Someone put planks across the swamp so we didn't get our feet too wet. When we reached the hot springs, all we found was a small wooden building almost like an outhouse. The hot springs could be seen by the steam coming off the creek. The springs actually bubbled up under the creek. We were the only two people there, so we took off our clothes and went skinny dipping. After several long, dusty days, this was like dying and going to heaven. What a great hot springs! We did not know, however, that grizzly bears liked using the hot springs also. There were many legends about the blue bears in the area and especially during the winter when the air was very cold, the bears would go into the hot springs. When they got out of the hot water, their fur would freeze and look blue to anyone seeing them under the moonlight. Fortunately for us, we saw no bears. Ignorance has its rewards.

After we left the hot springs, just a few miles down the road was a hand lettered sign saying: "homemade bread and jams". We were really getting low on food by then and we were also pretty hungry after our swim in the hot spring. The sign point-ed to a dirt trail off the main highway. We drove about one mile off the main road and came upon an old log cabin. Sign on the window said: "fresh bread". We went up to the door and a very kindly older Indian lady opened it and let us in. The smell inside her cabin made both of our mouth's water. Nothing else smells like fresh homemade bread. We bought two loaves and a jar of blueberry jam from her for about three dollars. I wish we could have afforded more. If I remember correctly, we had both loaves eaten and most of the jam gone within 100 miles of driving. When you are kids and you are hungry, you eat when you can and you eat what you have!

We crossed into the Yukon Territories twice that morning. The road makes a dip in and out of British Columbia and finally stays in the Territories farther north. The best part of the roads were the bridges. They were all paved except for a few with metal grates for a deck. The road itself went in and out of dust, wash board, mud and construction. I was so glad we had new tires on the car. Keith would drive for a while and then I would drive for a while. As the road droned on farther north, the more anxious we were to reach Alaska.

We stopped at a wide spot to camp which was not far out of Watson Lake, Yukon Territories. The next morning, we ate our breakfast and looked at the map which showed a lake just behind the campground. We decided we should check it out and try a little fishing. Of course, what's on a map compared with what's on the ground differed greatly. We walked for a long way through the woods before finding the lake and realized it was surrounded by swamp and billions of mosquitoes. It was very hard to get near an area to fish without wading far into the water. We skirted the lake for some time and we were surprised to find houses along one side of the lake. We kept walking toward the houses and finally came across a road which led back up to the highway. When we reached the highway, we discovered we were less than a mile from our car. We felt like we had walked five miles or more. Most likely we walked more miles then what we expected; maps can be very deceptive.

Before the day was over, we reached Whitehorse, Yukon Territories. Whitehorse is the largest city in the Yukon.

Whitehorse is actually the largest city between Fort St. John and Fairbanks, Alaska. We stocked up on gas and groceries and spent the night at a campground not far out of the city. When driving into Whitehorse, the road crosses the Yukon River. It's not really the starting point of the river but it is the farthest point up the Yukon River you can take a stern wheeler which is why Whitehorse has such strong roots with gold mining. The city of Whitehorse was the main jump off spot for miners as they searched for gold all over the Northern Territories and Alaska. If one was to float the Yukon River this would be the spot to put in your raft. Many miners did exactly that; built rafts along the river and then floated down to the mining fields all along the area. When Keith and I arrived in Whitehorse, it was a sleepy little town. We both were amazed at the size of Whitehorse as well as the deep, rich history of this small city where the railroad and the bus lines both come together.

Once we drove out of Whitehorse, the road became isolated again. By now we were far enough North to start experiencing frost heaves and frozen tundra. The road was mostly gravel but kept smooth by constant grading. Around Whitehorse some of the roads were actually paved, but this did not last long. As we continued our way North, we came to Haines Junction which is the turn off south to Haines, Alaska. We passed up the trip to Haines and continued North toward the Canadian/US border. A few miles South of Kluane Lake, we came across a road leading off to the right of the highway. We decided to follow the road to see where it would lead. To our surprise, it ended at a deserted Canadian Mounty Outpost. Everything was well preserved at that time. There were dog kennels, log cabins, and an old Model A car parked at the entrance of the town which almost looked like with a little work, it could run. The old car had wooden spokes on the wheels and the tires were still inflated. Keith and I were amazed by how well preserved this little outpost was at that time. We took lots of pictures before going back on the Alcan and heading North. We camped along Kluane Lake that night which is the largest lake in the Yukon. The size is like a small inland ocean. For a lake in which Keith and I had never heard of before, its size boggled our minds. During the time we were there, it was just wild country. We could see the large dahl sheep wandering around on the hills and the mountains above Kluane Lake. After dinner, we decided to climb up the mountain which was behind our campground. When we were up fairly high on the mountain, we found rocks which were balanced just on the edge of the mountain. We pushed one of them down the mountain and watched the rock bounce almost all the way to the road. We ended up pushing several more down the side which turned out to be a lot of fun. Today you wouldn't dare to do something like that.

4

WELCOME TO ALASKA

The next day we drove through Destruction Bay which is a small village located near the North end of Kluane Lake. During the trip, I thought the name "Destruction Bay" was interesting and I did not understand why or how the name was derived. I know now that in all the years I have driven the highway, this stretch of road is one of the worst along the whole highway. No matter how much work is done to improve the road it continues to fall apart at a rapid rate. We were positive we would blow a tire or break a spring on this stretch of the highway.

We finally made it to Beaver Creek, Yukon Territories which is the last village before entering Alaska. The U.S. Customs and Border Protection – Alcan Port of Entry is located just north of Beaver Creek at milepost 1221.8. As we drove to the Alcan Beaver Creek Border Crossing, about 30 miles between the Canadian Customs and the Alaska border, the road was terrible! We were so tired of wash board, potholes and frost heaves that seeing the Alaska border was like seeing a glass of water in a desert. When we reached the border, there was actually a sign and a concrete marker showing the exact line between America and Canada. The woods were cleared on both sides showing the boundary going out into infinity. We stopped there and took pictures of the welcome sign. We could see the U.S. Customs building about 300 yards up the hill from where we were. We jumped in the car and drove the last few feet up to the customs shack and were greeted by a very friendly customs man who welcomed us back into the United States. Once he saw how far we had come and what we had driven, he got a great big smile on his face. We pulled out of the customs crossing and into Alaska. The roads were paved and felt so smooth! Keith and I just started laughing, happy we had made it all the way to Alaska. Then we hit the first pothole in the paved road and we were sure we had broken the frontend right off the car. Potholes in pavement were much worse than potholes in gravel. We really had to slow down and watch out for the holes.

When Keith and I crossed the border into Alaska I knew I had found my home. The sky was a brilliant blue and the mountains were covered in snow. The colors of the foliage took my breath away. Lakes full of fish and rivers without names bigger than the Willamette River in Oregon. I know what Lewis and Clark must have felt like when they reached the Pacific Ocean. I knew at that moment that I would find a way to come back to Alaska.

We stopped that night at a small campground off the main road next to a lake. As soon as we arrived and set up our camp, I grabbed my fishing tackle and began fishing in the lake. Keith decided to stay back at the camp. I kept fishing down among the weeds and the willows. While I was fishing a game warden showed up. He pulled up to our camp and got out and started talking to Keith. He wanted to know if Keith had been fishing in the lake. Keith of course said no, which wasn't a lie. The game warden said he would need a fishing license to fish in this lake. Meanwhile I was having a great time fishing and was completely unaware of what was happening back at camp. The game warden hung around for several minutes and looked over our stuff pretty close. I can't imagine him not figuring out that Keith was not alone. He finally got back in his car and left at just about the same time I came up from the lake carrying our dinner. Keith had this real funny look on his face and then told me how close we came to getting caught. I was amazed that so far away from anything we would run into a game warden. Our first night in Alaska and we almost went to jail! Well, the fish were still good, so we cooked them for dinner destroying all evidence.

The next day we drove the remaining 275 miles to Fairbanks. We arrived in the afternoon and decided to splurge and get a motel room. We found some small log cabins along College Road. Fortunately, College Road was paved. In fact, Fairbanks had three paved roads when we got there. Almost all of Airport Way and College Road, as well as the Richardson Highway coming into town, were paved. There were also paved roads up at the University of Alaska. The log cabins were cute and not too expensive. Keith and I needed a shower and a decent bed to sleep in and the cabins fit the bill. We called home that night to tell our parents we had made it alive and had arrived in Fairbanks, Alaska. Of course, my dad wanted to know if I still had his credit card. I guess he wasn't too happy that I had taken it on the trip. I told him we would not use it unless we had an emergency. Fortunately, we never had an emergency nor did we ever need to use his credit card.

In those days, a phone call was very expensive. Keith and I called our parents collect and we had to keep it short. Still, each call was over $20. We told our parents how well things were going but I'm sure they were worried sick about us being so far from home in our little Ford coupe. We assured them the car was running just fine and we were making great time and great memories. They must have asked us both a dozen questions about the trip. They were able to live the adventure though us.

The next day we went around exploring Fairbanks. We found old wooden boardwalks along the Old Richardson Highway where it first came into Fairbanks which is now Cushman Street. Outside one of the bars along the road was a mule tied up to a hitching post. The mule was loaded with packs, bed rolls, gold pans and other miscellaneous gear. About the time we stopped to look at the mule, an old miner came out of the bar all bent over with his rifle on his arm. He wore a very wide brimmed floppy looking hat, he also had a full white beard which went down past his chest. He was right out of a Robert Service poem and made me feel like I had gone back in time 100 years. He untied the mule and started off down the street. Most likely he was headed back out into the bush to continue his mining. It was a sight I have never forgotten. This was by far the land of the last frontier.

We drove up to the University of Alaska campus and found a place with a scenic overlook pullout with a picture plaque of the mountains off in the distance. The plaque gave the names of the mountains we could see off in the distance on that clear sunny day. We had a great view of the Alaska Range although we could not see Mt. McKinley from there because it was farther south. Had we driven up on any hill with a clear view south, Mt. McKinley would have stood out all by itself. No doubt this is the largest mountain in North America. I had never seen skies so clear and blue and the fall colors took my breath away. The mountains looked so close I felt I could reach out and touch them. The University stood out with its modern buildings. In those days, the university was notorious for its mineral sciences and studies and one of the top schools for geology. Today the school offers so much more, with super computers, earth sciences, study of climate change, aviation, and many, many other subjects. The University of Alaska is one of the few Land, Sea and Space Grant universities in the country. It also has one of the most fascinating museums in the world.

We left Fairbanks and headed down the Richardson Highway toward Glennallen, Alaska. On the way, we followed the Gulkana River on the right side of the highway. During September, the pink salmon are spawning and are bright red. We stopped along the way and watched hundreds of salmon going upstream towards the high lakes. What a sight to see! There was so much bright red in one small river; Keith and I were just amazed at the number of fish we were seeing.

We turned off at Glennallen and headed toward Palmer, Alaska on the Glenn Highway. The scenery on this stretch of highway is incredibly beautiful. This was the first time we saw a glacier from the highway. Once through Palmer we continued on towards Anchorage. We stopped at a campground right outside of Anchorage and spent the night, then drove into Anchorage the next morning. The Great Alaska Earthquake happened one year prior on March 24, 1964 and the damage was still showing everywhere. The roads were under repair and many buildings were either being torn down or repairs were being made. I remember seeing the J. C. Penney's building and it looked like someone hit the corner of it with a large hammer and the building was cracked all over. Although the building was still standing, it looked really bad. We drove out the Seward Highway a few miles. The damage to the railroad track was still apparent with huge up and down lifts in the tracks and the rails were still bent in weird directions. There were still vehicles upside down on the side of Turnagain Arm and the roads were still at weird angles and with dips and dives everywhere. We took several pictures and knowing it had been a year since the quake, we were surprised at what was still left to repair. We talked to people we met along the way who had survived the quake. Their stories were amazing and I was surprised they still wanted to live in that area.

5

HEADING HOME

After we visited Anchorage, we decided we had better head home. We both wanted to drive farther south to Seward or even Homer, but when we counted the money we had left we had to face the fact that $94 was all we had of the $285 we started with. We quickly realized we had quite a challenge in front of us to make it home with less than $100, but we forged ahead with what little funds were in our pocket. It was getting to be late September and the weather could change at any time. We made it back to the border without any problems and we even made it all the way to Whitehorse, Yukon Territories by the second day. We knew the gas prices were really high between Whitehorse and the beginning of the highway, so every time we would come to a gas station, we would ask for only $5 worth of gasoline. We knew no one traveling on the highway ever passed a gas station without topping off, but the station attendant would top us off anyway even though we only asked them for $5 worth. Three separate times this happened to us and each time they would say it was their mistake and would take the $5 and let us leave with a full tank of fuel.

On the third night, somewhere between Whitehorse and Watson Lake, the rain started coming down. The road became super slick. We continued driving right on into the dark trying to make it to Watson Lake. The visibility dropped to almost nothing because of fog that came in right at the end of the rain. Two times, we almost hit a semi-truck coming at us since we could only see a few feet ahead of us. The road was so slick that we were crabbing the car towards the center of the road. Finally, we just had to give up. It was the scariest night of driving we had ever experienced. The next morning, we awoke to sunshine and drier roads. We drove about 75 miles before we realized I had left my coat back at the campground we stayed at the night before. We turned around and went back, but the coat was gone and we had just added 225 miles to our trip and another tank of fuel. It was a nice coat, but not that nice!

By the fourth day we were back at the turn off to Hudson's Hope, British Columbia. We were both tired but making great time although our money was nearly gone. I don't think we even stopped for food, but at least the gas prices were coming down. We stayed one night at some campground along the way and woke up to a noise in our heater of the car. We realized a mouse had moved in during the night. Every time we would turn on the blower motor, the little mouse would squeal at us until we turned off the heater. We had no way to get him out so we just put up with him for several days.

When we were getting close to the Canadian/American border, we realized we did not have enough money to make it home; we would need three more tanks of fuel. We decided on one more trick. We knew Americans would accept Canadian change, but not so with the Canadian dollars. Keith and I went into a store before we reached the border and converted all our Canadian dollars to Canadian change. It wasn't that much money, but it enabled us to stretch our trip all the way back to Milwaukie, Oregon where we lived.

When we crossed the border back into America, the U.S. Customs agent asked us if we had brought anything with us from Canada. We said yes we had brought a mouse back with us and we couldn't get it out of our heater vent. The guy looked at us like we were crazy so we turned on the blower motor for the heater and the mouse started squealing. The man just started laughing and told us to get going. I think he took one look at us and the car and figured we just needed to get home. That poor car was so dirty that trying to figure the color of the paint was almost impossible.

We filled up with gas just across the border and paid with our Canadian change. The guy was a little upset with us, but I figured once again he took one look at us and our car and thought these poor guys have been through a lot. We also told him that the change was all we had and he finally said OK and sent us on our way. We had to get gas one more time to make it to home. After that, we had a total of $1.50 left. When we got into Milwaukie, we stopped at a Dairy Queen and bought two milk shakes and then we were broke.

We headed home about two miles away. As we turned onto the last street, the car quit. The motor just died. We both got out of the car and walked the last block home. We walked into the house and yelled that we were home and dad came out and asked where was the car? I said the car didn't make it; died a block from the house. It turned out the fuel pump just quit and we had brought another fuel pump with us for the trip, but that fuel pump turned out to be the wrong one. I guess when I look back, we were just full of dumb luck.

When we arrived home, my draft notice was waiting for me. Keith, rather than being drafted into the service, joined the Air Force and Ray went into the National Guard. During January 1966, I went off to Fort Polk, Louisiana leaving behind my childhood, family and friends; none of our lives were ever the same once we separated and joined the military.

6

RETURN TO ALASKA ON THE BLADES OF A HELICOPTER

Although I was drafted into the Army, which could have meant infantry, I really felt that aviation would be more to my liking. So, I joined the Army specifically to get into aviation. I had the idea that it would lead me into fixed wing aircraft maintenance, but due to the Vietnam War, I was switched over to helicopter maintenance. It all started in Ft. Rucker, Alabama, which led to Ft. Eustis, Virginia and Chinook CH-47 school. I was then sent to Ft. Benning, Georgia, where I was assigned to a new company called the 242 Mule Skinners. We shipped out to Vietnam in early August 1967. At first we were assigned duty near Saigon, but soon they shipped us out to Chu Chi which is a small village in the center of the country. I was a Flight Engineer assigned to a specific aircraft where I was deeply involved in the aviation maintenance. Once or twice after being shot down, you are motivated to become a very good aircraft mechanic! I survived my year in country with only a few nicks and scratches.

In August 1968, I returned to America and the Pacific Northwest from Vietnam. I was honorably discharged from the Army on August 13, 1968. Like all Vietnam veterans returning from the war, I carried the scars and the confusion that went with such a difficult and morally strange war. Still the Army gave me a chance to use the G-I Bill, providing an opportunity to attend college. Since I already had training in aircraft maintenance, I figured it would be easy to get my civilian licenses. So, I went back to school in Portland, Oregon where I earned an Associate's Degree as well as my Airframe and Powerplant (A&P) mechanic's license. The A&P license allowed me to work on civilian aircraft anywhere in the United States.

Finding a job was not as easy back then because of all the returning veteran pilots and mechanics who entered the field of aviation. Vietnam had been the first war where the helicopter became the workhorse for the military. After a long search, I found a job in Boise, Idaho at a company called Inter Mountain Helicopters. I spent the summer of 1971 working in New Mexico in the Capitan National Forest fighting fires with a Bell G3-B1 helicopter. I traveled all over the state as well as parts of Arizona and fell in love with that area of our country, however, Alaska was always on my mind.

After leaving Idaho in the Fall of 1971, I found a job with Columbia Construction Helicopters at Swan Island in Portland, Oregon. I met Gordon MacDonald, a feisty young helicopter pilot not unlike myself. At first he was unsure of my skills as a mechanic. We were both sent to Parkdale, Oregon with a Hiller FH-1100 turbine helicopter to support the larger operations of Columbia Construction Helicopters. They were one of the only companies in the country who flew Boeing Vertol helicopters. They were operating the converted Marine Ch-46 civilian tandem rotor helicopters. They could lift quite a load and the company was using them for helicopter long line logging. Gordon and I were put up in a 24-foot travel trailer located in a trailer park just outside of town. Gordon owned a 1967 Camaro with a 350 engine. The car was running very rough and had little power so I took the carburetor off and rebuilt it. Then the car would go really fast but would not idle. Gordon was having his doubts about my skills. Well, it just so happened there was an old auto maintenance shop in Parkdale, so I stopped by and talked to an old guy in greasy overalls. I told him my problem and he immediately asked me if the engine was a 327 or a 350. I said a 350. He asked me if I had kept the bottom gasket to the old carburetor. The only rebuild kits available were for the 327 which was missing the bottom gasket for the 350 because it needed another hole to fit the 350 carburetor. I rushed back to the trailer park and saw that the garbage truck had not come by yet. I dove into the dumpster and dug to the bottom and found the old gasket. I pulled off the carburetor and reinstalled the old gasket. I was just putting the carburetor back on the engine when Gordon got back from flying. I told him I fixed his car. He jumped in, gave it gas and he peeled rubber and shot out of the trailer park like a cat on fire. His car ran perfectly and from then on he had no more doubts about my mechanical abilities. I never told him the whole story!

After a short time, we became the best of friends and developed a working relationship that lasted until his untimely death in 1983 when a building collapsed on him. Gordon was an extraordinary individual with a huge heart and I was the most privileged person to have been his friend.

Columbia Construction Helicopters was involved with many worldwide endeavors. Long line logging got me out into the woods. The pay was poor and like most aircraft mechanics, I was always looking for another job with better pay but mostly I just wanted to go north to Alaska.

I stayed on with Columbia Construction Helicopters through the winter. Gordon worked only the summer with Columbia Construction Helicopters and then he traveled down to California where he found work with a company called Briles Wing and Helicopter. Briles had just bought out a company in Alaska called Tundra Copters. They hired Gordon to ferry a helicopter from California to Alaska and work a job out on the Aleutian Chain of Alaska in the small community of Port Heiden. The job was very remote, the work was hard and Gordon's mechanic soon quit. Gordon called me via short wave radio and asked if I would be interested in coming to Alaska to be his mechanic again. As luck would have it, I had just given my two-week notice at Columbia Construction Helicopters. They were not happy that I quit the company, so they fired me. After Gordon called me, I flew to Alaska the next day. I arrived in Fairbanks, Alaska in the late afternoon and I was picked up by the Director of Maintenance, Walt Whitehorn, of Tundra Copters. He was quite a character and after a very short time at the office while filling out the necessary paperwork, he gave me a tour of the local bar. I remember waking up at three in the morning and thinking it was four in the afternoon – 24 hours of daylight will do that to you in the Land of the Midnight Sun!

The next day I was loaded on a Wein Airlines flight to Anchorage. I then caught a flight on a DC-3 owned and operated by Reeve Aleutian Airlines. This was a very rough flight and several people got sick while we were flying over the mountains. I was more than glad to get off the plane in Port Heiden, Alaska. I can only say I was a bit "green" flying with all those sick passengers.

I realized I was finally back in Alaska. The area I found myself in was unlike anything I had ever imagined. The sand dunes and rolling, wind-swept grass went on for miles. There were many pot hole lakes and streams with rivers coming out of the mountains to the North which bordered the Northern side of the Aleutian Chain. Gordon met me at the airport and quickly loaded me onto the helicopter taking me for a quick test flight over the area. We flew over large moose with huge racks, large grizzly bears and abundant water fowl. After that flight, not a day went by without seeing wildlife of every kind.

Port Heiden is a small fishing community in Alaska so there were numerous boats and fishermen during that time of year. Gordon and I stayed at the work camp for several weeks and while there, we helped out whenever we could. One of our side trips was to sling load a large industrial refrigerator from a camp out in the woods back to the cook shack at Port Heiden. One thing you learn when you are staying in the field is to take care of the camp cooks no matter what. The refrigerator was very heavy and almost an hour-long flight from the base camp. Of course, the second we picked up the refrigerator, the wind began to blow fairly hard. This turned into a very risky flight back to camp. The cook was so excited to see the refrigerator arrive that he fed us steak that night. In fact, he took very good care of Gordon and me the whole time we were out there.

We were scheduled to leave Port Heiden and fly to Cordova, Alaska. Just before our scheduled day of departure, one of the geologists we were supporting tossed a rock hammer through the blades while the helicopter was running. It was an accident, but it severely damaged the rotor blade it made contact with. The company had to fly in a new rotor blade to us which took a few days. The company had another helicopter in the area which was scheduled to fly North to Circle City, Alaska which is a very small village located North of Fairbanks on the Yukon River. Because of our delay, the company decided to switch aircraft destinations and the airworthy helicopter was sent to Cordova, Alaska instead of us since I had to repair the other helicopter when the parts arrived. Once the aircraft was repaired, we flew North 2,000 miles in a straight line without leaving the state and we headed to Circle City. We carried full 5-gallon cans of fuel on the cargo racks. We would stop along the way and put fuel in the aircraft so we could reach the next village where fuel was available. Along the way, we landed in a very remote village. We were the first to land a helicopter there. I think everyone in the village came down to check us out. The village missionary was the only person there who spoke English. He came down to where we had landed and told us we were in the first flying machine these people had ever seen. At first, the people were very shy, but the kids were soon climbing around on the cargo racks which gave the adults a little more courage. They were very nice people and in the end, everyone waved at us when we took off. For Gordon and me it was a once in a lifetime experience.

The helicopter was flying with an unusually bad bounce when Gordon lowered the collective. We decided to stop in Fairbanks where we had the maintenance hangar. It turned out the hammer had also damaged the bearing in the rotor head, so I had to take it apart and replace the bearings and sleeves before we could continue on to Circle City, Alaska.

In years past, Circle City actually had a trail south 165 miles to Fairbanks. At that time, Circle City was the farthest North log cabin town in Alaska and was the jump off point for gold miners coming out of the gold fields located upriver on the Yukon. The old stern wheelers would dock at Circle and the miners would resupply and enjoy the bars. In those days, the town supported over 600 log cabins and hundreds of individuals who lived there. The trail was built to the new settlement of Fairbanks located on the Tanana River. During that time, Fairbanks was the farthest North on the Tanana River where the steam operated sternwheelers could travel. Consequently, Fairbanks became a huge supply depot and mail center for the miners up North. Once Felix Pedro found gold not far out of Fairbanks, things changed in a hurry and the small town of Circle began to shrink. By the time Gordon and I arrived in Circle City, the town was a sleepy little community of Indian and white folks and the trail to Fairbanks had become a dirt road used only in the summer and was closed during the winter.

Gordon and I finished our summer contract at the town of Circle where we both enjoyed our time more than we realized. The setting for Circle City was located right on the Yukon River. The midnight sun was beautiful and the 24 hours of daylight took some getting used to. It was here where I met the future mother of my two boys. She was the daughter of Frank and Mary Warren; they owned the Yukon Trading Post. Her name was Vickie and she was a very pretty but shy young lady. Gordon and I stayed with the contract crew in one of Frank's log cabin bunkhouses. We ate our meals at the Yukon Trading Post Restaurant where Vickie was working for her parents. I saw her nearly every day and soon we started a friendship.

After the summer of 1972, I left Tundra Copters and returned to Oregon. I kept in touch with Vickie and soon she decided to travel to Oregon where I was renting a house. After a short time, we decided to return to Alaska and get married in Circle City at the Yukon Trading Post. I owned a Mazda RX-3 and Vickie and I drove from Portland to Fairbanks in late October. We were married on my mother's birthday, November 5, 1972, by a Ft. Yukon magistrate in Circle City, Alaska. I remember the cold and the dark and the temperature was hovering around 30 below zero the day we got married. People flew in from all over the state. You could not drive to Circle City because the road was closed for the winter. Everyone enjoyed the party in the basement of the Trading Post. The bar was open, drinks were free and several people, including the magistrate, were drunk by the time the wedding began. Alaska was really a wild and free country! Vickie and I drove to Oregon after our wedding, but it was not long before we both wanted to live in Alaska. So, we traded in the Mazda and bought a 1973 Ford pick-up truck and a 29 foot fifth-wheel trailer. Vickie and I left Oregon in February 1973 and drove up to Fairbanks. The road had been improved considerably since my trip in 1965, but was still an adventure. The Alcan Highway was always under construction and was still very windy. When we drove into the Yukon Territories, we spent the night at Watson Lake. The outside temperature had been dropping all night. We were awakened very early in the morning because the heater in the trailer was not working and we were both freezing. The reason the heater was not working was because propane cannot flow when the temperature is colder than forty below zero and that morning, the temperature was fifty-two degrees below zero. The truck would not start and we were bundled up in about every coat we owned. We finally got help from a local garage where they had a Master Heater which directed the heat under the truck engine. We also put a few blankets over the hood of the truck to help get the engine warm enough so after about an hour we were able to start the truck -- we never turned the engine off again until we reached Fairbanks. That was by far the coldest trip I have ever been on.

7

INTRODUCTION TO
THE AMBLER RIVER

After our return to Fairbanks, I found a job with Merrick Helicopters as a Field Mechanic on helicopters. In early summer, they sent me North to the small village of Arctic Village, Alaska. I worked there until the birth of my son, Fred, who was born on Flag Day, June 14, 1973. I stayed in town for only a short time and was then sent out with a Hiller 12E flown by a grizzly old Hiller pilot by the name of Ray Houseman. Ray had actually flown Hiller Helicopters with "Old Man Hiller" himself. Ray was by far the best Hiller pilot I had ever worked with. He was hard to get along with and get to know, but eventually we both earned respect for each other. Merrick sent us Northwest to Dahl Creek Airstrip located near Kobuk, Alaska. We refueled and then went over the mountains into the Ambler River Valley. We were sent there to support Sunshine Mining Company where they were surveying, taking samples, and staking mineral claims in the area of the Western Brooks Range looking for gold, copper and other minerals of any value.

Finding myself in this part of the world was like no other place I had known. This place was going to change my soul for the rest of my life. It was here, in the Brooks Range, that the story really begins and my life would become part of the Ambler River forever.

The Sunshine Mining camp was your typical wilderness tent village. There was a cook tent, supply tent, mineral shop tent which contained all the maps, samples, staking equipment and a dining activity tent. There were also several two-man sleeping tents and one tent I used for helicopter support. The camp was located on a small rise among willows very near the river. The river itself had very clear water and one could look all the way to the bottom and see the many colored rocks. You could actually see the fish swimming along. The valley ran North to South in that area and was fairly wide but narrowed the farther North you went. To the North, the valley entered into the Brooks Range and when the sun shined upon those mountains to the North it was like time stood still and everyone in the camp would just stop and stare at the beauty that surrounded us; of course, the mosquitoes surrounded us, too! To the South, the valley opened up to the Shungnak River Valley and off in the distance beyond the Shungnak River is the small range of mountains ahead of the Kobuk River Valley. At the foot of those mountains, in a straight line down the Ambler, sat the Bornite Mine. The mine was outfitted with its own airstrip, maintenance shop, first class living quarters and a large cafeteria with cooking facilities.

When Ray and I arrived, we landed the helicopter on a high gravel bar upstream from the camp. The area was very open with great approaches from all directions. I found an area not too far from the helicopter to put my toolbox, ladders and support supplies. We had several 55 gallon drums of fuel and a hand pump located near the helicopter. Since the camp was new, there was still a lot of work in progress and several of the shelters were in the process of being built. We helped clear brush for tent sites where paths were made from tent to tent. We dug out a spot for an outhouse and an area to put our garbage. Chainsaws, generators, propane tanks, tables and chairs were all needed to support the camp. All in all, there were about 13 people in the camp which consisted of geologists, assistant geologists, surveyors, helpers, camp cooks, a camp boss and of course, the pilot and me. The tents were wood framed with a canvas floor, roof and sides. Summer in Alaska is beautiful with hot afternoons and cool evenings. When working to put a camp together, good old American ingenuity plays a huge roll. We needed a shower, so we placed it on a gravel bar near the camp. Just a wood frame with Visqueen plastic sheeting around it and a five gallon can mounted on top of it. The can had a shower nozzle mounted on the bottom and a propane torch under the can. We had a couple of girls in the camp, so privacy was important for them. When you wanted to take a hot shower, you would fill the five-gallon container with water from the river, start the propane torch and if timed right, you could have a nice warm shower or a hot shower if you waited too long.

We also decided we needed a sauna. We built a small shelter into the river bank about 30 feet away from the river. We gathered up several large rocks and made a fire pit. We would use another container to pour water onto the rocks once they were hot which produced a lot of steam. This was more of a sweat lodge but it worked! We made a clear path to the river so when it was time to cool down, it was easy to just run and jump into the very cold water of the river. This was a great camp and the weather was perfect for the first several weeks we were there. The weather stayed so dry we began to think we might need to move the shower because the river level went down, but we never needed to do so.

A typical day began around six o'clock in the morning. The days were near 24 hours of daylight so flying in the dark was not a worry. The helicopter could only hold two people plus the pilot, so several trips were required to get everyone out in the field. By eight o'clock in the morning, the camp would be virtually empty and only the camp cook and I would remain. They worked six days a week with Sunday being the off day which gave the crew a much-needed rest. This also provided me with the opportunity to work on the helicopter. I would constantly maintain the helicopter in the evening, but some maintenance required more time, so that one day off was used for the heavier inspections. Weekends were used for sleep, letter writing and, of course, the more dedicated geologists would spend time mapping mineral samples. One fellow brought a unicycle to camp and everyone would try their skills at riding it. In the evening after dinner, the crew would get together for a few card games and storytelling. We kept in contact with the outside world with a very powerful single sideband radio. I was in charge of the radio during the day when the helicopter was out of camp. If any accident would happen, I would contact Anchorage emergency and within a short time, a rescue was on the way. I took that part of my job very seriously and twice that summer I was put in the position of organizing a rescue of an injured man in the field.

The camp was supplied weekly by flights out of Fairbanks to Dahl Creek or Bornite. Ray and I would fly the helicopter into either of these two strips and pick up supplies and the mail for the whole camp. This was always an exciting day when the mail was delivered. All trips out of camp were used to deliver the mail going out as well as taking the rock samples to be analyzed back at the company lab. Some trips out would carry empty propane tanks and empty fuel barrels would be sling loaded out to be refueled and returned.

We went through a lot of fuel and my arms became quite strong from using a hand pump to transfer all the fuel into the helicopter. We also had five-gallon aviation gas cans in wood crate boxes. Two gas cans to a box would be carried on the cargo racks of the helicopter which provided longer flying range capabilities. The empty wooden crates were in great demand at the camp because they made great shelves and storage boxes in the cook tent.

One thing about being a helicopter mechanic was you were also the camp mechanic. I fixed anything and everything from generators, stoves, lawn chairs, cameras and other miscellaneous tools. During the day when the helicopter was out flying and I was alone in camp, I would grab my fishing pole, which I took everywhere with me in Alaska, and go fishing. I carried a hand-held radio so if anything came up in camp while I was gone, I could run back down the river to camp to save the day. In the area, there were black bears and grizzly bears as well as moose. So I always carried my .41 Mag Ruger Blackhawk pistol with me. The story goes that the first five shots you use on the bear, if he still is coming at you, the last round was for yourself. We also wore bells on our person. They say the noise of a bell will keep you from startling any large animals should you walk into them. You could always tell the black bear scat from the grizzly bear scat by the bells found in the grizzly bear scat. I never had a problem with bears or moose while I was out fishing. Usually the mosquitoes were the greatest aggravation. Fishing on the river was probably like fishing in the pioneer days. I loved to fly fish and there were times I would catch several fish without getting my fly on water. The fish were jumping out of the water to get the fly before it got to the water. Arctic Grayling, the native fish for most of the Alaska streams, was plentiful and there was also Arctic Char and an occasional Sheefish. The Sheefish traveled mostly up the larger Kobuk River but since the Ambler River flowed into the Kobuk River, a few Sheefish would get lost. The solitude while out fishing was amazing. I knew I was the first person to ever fish some of those ripples. There was not a sound except the birds and the river – oh, and the buzz of just a few mosquitoes. I could always hear the helicopter returning from way off in the distance and I usually made it back to camp by the time Ray was shutting the helicopter down.

In the valley at night while it was so quiet around the campfire, we would often hear a deep rumble coming down the valley from up river or back behind us in the mountains. It was a few years later that I learned the sound was from rock slides echoing out of the mountains of the Brooks Range. But at the time when I was in the Sunshine Mining Camp, I would tell everyone that Indian legend spoke of the Great Buffoon up in the mountains and the Great Buffoon was angry which was the reason we would hear the rumbles. The truth, however, was the local Indians believed the valley was haunted and they did not like going up this particular river. Of course, every time I brought up the Great Buffoon, Ray would always back me up and even elaborate on the importance of the legend. We would sit around the campfire and talk half the night away about all the mysteries connected to Alaska.

About two weeks after we started talking about the Great Buffoon theory, the weather changed and the rains started, at times very heavy. The rain went on for days, the helicopter was grounded and delivery of our supplies and mail came to a halt. We played a lot of cards and read a lot of books. One night after everyone had gone to bed, the rain came down a lot harder than we expected and the river came up fast. The river water was already high, but this put it over its banks. We were all awakened by water running through our camp. We had to wade out into the river to save the helicopter because the water was up to the cargo racks. Several people woke up to water flowing through their tents. The cook tent was flooded but still there. Not so lucky was the shower and one of our empty fuel drums which got swept away down the river never to be seen again. We lost some of our supplies that night and most everything was soaked. It was a small disaster for our summer camping adventure and a major score for the Great Buffoon. It was the lowest point in everyone's morale. The rain and clouds continued to roll through for days. It was hard to dry out sleeping bags, tents and clothing, and at the same time move the whole camp to higher ground. Finally, the cold, damp weather let up and the sun broke through the clouds. It was as if someone turned on a light switch and everyone began to feel better. Our supplies and mail were delivered and that night we drank wine and ate steak and everyone laughed about the Great Buffoon.

Sometime in early August, I hiked up the river to go fishing at one of my favorite spots. It was a cloudy afternoon and at a particular area I liked to fish which was from a 30-foot high cliff which went down to the river into a deep swirling pool. The river was running south into this bank and made for a deep hole and a whirlpool at the base of the cliff. I had fished there before and the fish always seemed to fight over a good fly. The cliff itself jutted out into the river so there was a view both up and down the river. I had always thought this spot would be a great place for a cabin. Great view, high enough above the river to avoid flooding and yet access to clean water and southern exposure. I had already caught several fish, but I was playing the old catch and release game and as I was removing a fish off my hook, out of the corner of my eye, I spotted something out of the ordinary in the woods. There was something shiny on one of the few trees on the point. I let the fish go and walked over to investigate. There was a jar nailed to the tree with a note inside. I unscrewed the jar and read the note which indicated someone in the last couple of days had claimed the point and the surrounding five acres of land. I couldn't believe what I was seeing. I had been there all summer and didn't know the valley was open to recreational homesteading. I knew right then and there that I wanted a piece of this great and beautiful valley. I took off down river toward the camp and stopped at several spots which I thought would be good cabin sites only to find they were also staked. The writing was in the same handwriting so I figured someone had floated down the river and staked all the good spots for friends and neighbors. I was very disappointed. Later in the evening when I got back to camp, I told Ray what I had discovered and how disappointed I felt. Ray told me not to worry because we had something better than a canoe, and we needed to test fly the helicopter the next day since it was Sunday. We planned to go see what we could find.

The next day we flew down the river where the valley widened out. There was a point of rock which stretched out into the river. During high water, it was rapids. At first I thought it was too close to the water level, but Ray pointed out that just around the bend, the river bank climbed up quite a distance. He also pointed out that the view from the spot on the bank went almost 15 miles down the valley to the south where you could see the Kobuk mountains off in the distance. Another great feature was the gravel bar out front. This would make a perfect place for landing an airplane. The trees on the acreage were huge considering how far North we were and the ground was very level making this a great place to build. I spent some time pacing out an estimated five acres and put corner posts in the ground. I brought my camera and a jar from camp. I took pictures, wrote my claim, put it in the jar and nailed it to the biggest tree I could find which was closest to the river. Ray, being the older and wiser man, said this was the best spot of all the spots and in the end, I agreed he was right.

After all that, I still needed to file my claim with the Bureau of Land Management (BLM) office in Fairbanks. This all sounded so simple and I could not have guessed the extent of hardship I would need to complete in order to meet the requirements to prove up on the land, nor did I realize the Homestead Act was about to end.

The season came to a close near the end of September. Snow was in the air and the wind blowing down from the North and through our camp chilled us to the bone. Breaking down a large camp is quite a task and took several trips with the helicopter to get everything moved to the airstrip so it could be shipped out. After the camp was cleaned up, there was no evidence we had ever been there. We all said our goodbyes and Ray and I loaded the helicopter with my toolbox, our fly away kit and our personal effects such as sleeping bags, clothes and my guitar. The helicopter was loaded to the max. We flew from there to Bettles where we refueled and then flew on to Fairbanks.

Once in Fairbanks, I headed to the BLM office where I filed my claim for the Ambler River Homestead. Just filing the paperwork didn't make it mine and there were several hoops I needed to go through.

I had a total of five years to "prove up" on the land. Since I was a Veteran, this helped augment the minimum requirement of living on the land from three years to a five month stay. I still had to show I used the land in some capacity during the first three years of my claim. I then had to be living there before the end of the fifth year for at least five months. Since I dated my claim five months previous, this gave me only four years and seven months to make all the requirements come together. The site was located 395 miles Northwest from Fairbanks where there are no roads, railroads, or airstrips within 15 miles of the homestead. Consequently, this made a real hardship to prove up on this recreational homestead.

Back in Fairbanks, I began building a new house in the spring of 1974. I was working at Tundra Helicopters again, but now as their Director of Maintenance. Gordon was also working at Tundra Helicopters as their Chief Pilot and Director of Operations. In the Fall of 1974, I decided I needed to get my airplane up from Oregon. I asked Gordon if he would fly it up from Oregon if I paid for the trip down and back. The airplane was a 1946 Taylorcraft BC-12 D. I purchased the aircraft with three other individuals while going to aviation school and we used the aircraft as our school project. The four of us completely rebuilt the aircraft from the airframe to the powerplant. The engine was a Continental 65 horsepower with four cylinders. We bored out the cylinders to increase the horsepower to a whopping 75 horsepower. It was a fabric aircraft so we replaced all the fabric on the airplane and we painted the aircraft a beautiful sky blue with white stripes. This was a great project and a great learning experience for the four of us. As things would happen, one of the partner's health went downhill and he could not be involved in the ownership of the aircraft any longer, so he sold out of his quarter. Another partner moved away and sold his quarter to me and Bill Mickley as the last two remaining partners. Bill Mickley was having marital problems, so before his divorce he sold his half of the aircraft to me. Suddenly I was the sole owner of the airplane. However, I still had no pilot license, but Gordon did. I bought Gordon a ticket to fly to Portland where he met up with Bill Mickley. They went out to the airplane and Bill changed the oil and filter, ran the airplane and then let Gordon fly it around the patch for a test flight. The aircraft did not come with a radio but one was required to go through Canada so we purchased a portable Genave radio in order for Gordon to talk to the towers. After all the expenses and preparation, Gordon packed up his survival gear and headed North to Alaska. He had a successful trip except for one breakdown in which Gordon was forced to land on the Alaska Highway because the engine quit. The one fuel line going to the carburetor broke. The plane was near Watson Lake, Yukon Territories and Gordon was able to get a part to fix the problem. After being gone for almost 30 days, the plane and Gordon arrived safely in Fairbanks.

In the Spring of 1975, Gordon and I decided over a beer one afternoon that we should start our own helicopter business. Things had come to an end at Tundra Copters, I was fired and Gordon quit all in the same hour, so we had some time to dedicate to future opportunities. A few year earlier, Gordon had been involved in a very bad auto accident in Whitehorse, Canada. He had flown down to see his family in Pennsylvania and pick up his vintage 1957 Chevrolet two door coupe. On the way back to Fairbanks, he was hit head-on in a snowstorm in whiteout conditions just outside of Whitehorse, Yukon Territories. The accident shattered his right knee cap and almost ended his flying career. The doctors told Gordon his flying days were over, but Gordon would never give up and with a constant regiment of therapy on his knee as well as lots of heavy drinking, he overcame the disability. It took him almost two years, but he finally got his helicopter endorsement back.

In the Fall of 1975, I realized time was running out to prove up on my homestead. Although Gordon couldn't fly helicopters, he could fly an airplane. I explained the situation to

Gordon and convinced him that we needed to take a couple of weeks off and fly up to the cabin site. We needed to build a small shelter and clear some land. I also needed to take some pictures to show the BLM that I had been at the site and had made some improvements since I had staked the property. It was August and the weather could be unpredictable at that time of year in Alaska. Still Gordon and I felt we should give it a try using my old Taylorcraft.

When we left Fairbanks, the weather wasn't bad. We heard the weather was iffy up North, so we headed somewhat southwest toward the village of McGrath, Alaska. We figured then we would go North toward the cabin. We made it to McGrath without any issues. We refueled the aircraft and checked the weather up North. It wasn't that good but with a ceiling of 400 feet we felt we could follow the Koyokuk River, make it to the Kobuk Valley and then on to the cabin site. We left McGrath around two in the afternoon and as we flew North following the river, the cloud ceiling began to lower below 300 feet. The wind was also becoming a problem and was tossing the light, little airplane around like a kite. One other problem was the only instrument for direction, our compass, had become unreliable because of the iron in the mountains we were flying through. We both realized we needed to land and sit this one out. We were getting very close to Hughes, Alaska, so as the sky was coming down, I had my eyes peeled looking for the village. We were just about to give up and land on a gravel bar when I spotted the village and the airstrip. We landed there about 4PM. Both of us were exhausted from the tension and worry of potentially not making it.

The town of Hughes is a very small village located in the foothills of the Koyokuk River Valley. When we arrived, we noticed that the only people to come out and see what was happening were the elders and the children of the village. We found out there had been a forest fire in the area not too long ago and the firefighters who lived in the village had just been paid. They had taken their boats and went up river to Bettles, Alaska, to buy supplies for the winter as well as a few bottles of booze. The chief of the village was a very nice older gentleman who invited us to stay in his cabin for the night and have dinner with him. We brought sleeping bags with us so we agreed it would be better than a tent.

Sometime during the night, the young men of the village returned from their trip up stream to Bettles. They had been drinking on the way back and were pretty toasted by the time they arrived in Hughes. Our first indication of issues came about two o'clock in the morning when the cabin door burst open and three very drunk men came stumbling in, tripping over Gordon and me in the dark. Once they realized there were visitors in the cabin, they began yelling at us to drink with them. Gordon tried to convince them otherwise, but to no avail. Finally, we took a swig of their whiskey, hoping they would leave us alone. Not so! In their minds, the party was just beginning. When we refused more drinks, they started getting angry and I was sure we were in for a fight. The village chief finally convinced them to leave his cabin. The rest of the night, sleep was out of the question. They never went to bed and continued to whoop and holler throughout the rest of the night. We hoped when we got up in the morning that they would be passed out or asleep somewhere, but that was not the case. They were all wide awake, more drunk than before and out of booze. As soon as they saw us come out of the cabin, they surrounded us and wanted us to fly to Bettles and buy more whiskey. When we refused, they got very hostile and threatened to kill us. To this day I don't think they were joking. They offered us money which we refused and we convinced them we would go to Bettles, buy the whiskey and they could reimburse us on our return. It took us awhile to convince them we would be back, but finally they agreed.

They were all hanging around the aircraft making it hard for us to get ready to go. Gordon was finally able to get into the aircraft and I walked around front and cleared them away from the propeller. Once the plane started, they jumped away from the plane. I climbed into the passenger seat and belted myself in. Gordon taxied out onto the runway for takeoff. There was one major problem, however. The weather had not changed and in fact, was a little worse. We were afraid to go back to the village, figuring they would kill us if we did, so our only option was to take off. Gordon told me not to worry because the old man in the village told him about a pass through the mountains not far from the village which would take us into the Kobuk Valley. He told Gordon that Sam White, a historic bush pilot who lived in Hughes for many years, told him about the pass and how he used it in bad weather to get out of the valley. He described the pass to Gordon and told him what to look for once we were in the air.

The fog and clouds were close to river level, with banks and mountains on both sides of the river. We found ourselves flying by feel. Not a good way to fly. Still I could just make out the passes on the left side of the aircraft. Gordon told me to count to the third pass and this would be the one we would turn up. It wasn't long, maybe 10 minutes into the flight, when I saw the third pass. Gordon turned the plane into the pass and we were surprised at how fast the visibility improved. Once through the pass, the valley opened up and we had plenty of visibility. What a wise man Sam Bush must have been – he didn't die in an airplane crash! Gordon and I just thanked the Lord for his wisdom and for our lives.

It was still very early in the morning so we decided to continue on past the village of Kobuk and on to the Bornite airstrip at the start of the Ambler Valley. The weather was still a little iffy and when we landed at Bornite, we noticed several aircraft, including helicopters, located on the end of the strip. We parked the Taylorcraft and walked to the Bornite cafeteria where everyone was having breakfast. When we walked in, all eyes turned and looked at us. We knew several of the pilots and they all wanted to know where we had come from. I guess they had been stranded there for several days due to the bad weather. When we told them of our little adventure and that the weather was still bad, they all agreed we were beyond crazy. After they were nice enough to give us breakfast, we all sat around and told stories. One thing pilots have is lots of stories.

We ended up staying there for two days enjoying the hospitality of the Bornite Palace. On the third morning, we noticed the Ambler River Valley had a fairly high cloud ceiling and we could almost see all the way to the cabin site. Gordon told the other pilots we were going to make a run up the valley and would get back with them if the weather looked any better. We still had the small VHF radio on board, so we could communicate with them if we landed near the homestead. Gordon and I bought some more fuel from the mine and then checked over the aircraft. Once again, I hand-cranked the propeller and the aircraft started right up. We took off from Bornite for the ten-minute flight out to the homestead. We made a safe landing on a gravel bar right next to the land I had staked. We spent the day building a lean-to, took several pictures and paced off the acreage a lot more accurately then I had done a few years before. We were surprised that out in the old river bed, just in front of the land, was the old shower and the barrel that went missing during the Great Buffoon. I took pictures and included those as proof that I had been there before and used the land. We spent the night there in our little lean-to and I must admit, it was very quiet, and I think we both slept pretty well even though there were bears in the area. The next morning, we woke up to bright sunshine and clear skies. A few of the guys flew over us on their way back to work. We waved at them as they passed over to let them know we were fine. We stayed a while longer enjoying the sunshine before we loaded up the aircraft with our camping gear and headed back to Fairbanks.

When we returned to Fairbanks, I went back to the BLM office and filled out some more paperwork. I paid a small fee to record the claim officially. It would be a year before I could return.

8

STARTING SUNSHINE HELICOPTERS

Gordon was a very good businessman and pilot. I knew helicopters and how to keep them flying. It made for a great partnership. Gordon found out that the military was going to auction off several older training helicopters in Arizona. They were Hiller 12-D and Hiller 12-E aircraft. He flew down to Arizona and used his settlement money from the auto accident in Whitehorse, Yukon Territories, Canada, to buy two helicopters. One D model and one E model. The only difference between the two helicopters were the size of the engines. The D model had a Lycoming VO 435 engine and the E model had a VO 540 engine. The auction almost depleted all of Gordon's money, and we still needed to ship them to Alaska. Gordon had to hire a shipping company to crate up the helicopters and have them freighted to Alaska. It took all the money we had left to get them to Fairbanks. Once we got them up to Fairbanks, Gordon was able to raise an additional $20,000 to get one of them to fly and we began Sunshine Helicopters.

Once the helicopters arrived we moved them out to my place in Fairbanks. I lived outside of town about 20 miles. My house was in a very wooded area but there was a clear area in front of the house. After going over the records on the two helicopters we decided that getting the D model up and flying would be the easiest and the quickest. The aircraft had low time on all the components and the airframe was low time as well. The aircraft serial number indicated it was built to civilian standards which made it easy to get a standard airworthiness certificate from the Federal Aviation Administration (FAA).

I spent the summer of 1975 inspecting, rebuilding and painting the aircraft. Once I was ready to fly the aircraft I contacted the FAA so they could come inspect the aircraft and the paperwork. They approved the aircraft for the standard airworthiness certificate. We test flew the helicopter right out of my back yard. Made a few adjustments and then flew it into Fairbanks and landed at the Fairbanks Airport. This was a great day! Gordon and I now had a helicopter to fly and Gordon finished getting a Part 135 certificate for the company which allowed us to transport passengers and cargo for revenue. He just had to complete his check ride with the FAA in the helicopter to officially become the Chief Pilot and President of Sunshine Helicopters.

**Hiller D Model Helicoper and
the Dog Named "Moose"**

Gordon also spent some time looking for work. We decided to base our company in Circle City, Alaska. Consequently, Sunshine Helicopters became the farthest north helicopter company in Alaska. We started out supporting gold miners, some outdoor adventures and a few BLM fire contracts. It was a meager beginning and I had to go back to work at Wein Airlines that winter to keep the bills paid. Gordon went to work during the winter with R&M Consultants. That only lasted until the beginning of Summer 1976. The Trans-Alaska Pipeline System was being built and helicopters were in great demand. Suddenly, we began to get very busy with overflow work.

We needed storage for the aircraft and space to do maintenance. We decided we needed to build a hangar, so Gordon hired a friend of his, Dick Bush, who was an architect and a builder. He designed a hangar for us to be built in Circle City. We were able to lease some land from my father-in-law, Frank Warren. With Dick's help, and several other folks including Gordon and me, the hangar was built. After the hangar was built, the company began to grow. To our surprise, we picked up some major contracts located in our area. We had to expand, so we bought our first new helicopter, a Hughes 500-C model. It was the last 500-C off the production line. Soon we had five helicopters and we were hiring help for the summer months. We just kept growing and we soon needed crew quarters to house our employees. Frank Warren was ready to sell the Yukon Trading Post, so Gordon made arrangements to buy the Trading Post, bunkhouse, motel, liquor store, post office, bar, restaurant and the gas pumps. He also bought Frank and Mary Warren's house and the maintenance garage. Basically, Gordon bought 75% of all the commercial buildings in Circle, Alaska.

9

AIRPLANES AND MARY

In the summer of 1976, I started flying my Taylorcraft aircraft. One of the pilots, Tim Jahn, who was stationed in Circle City and was flying in and out of Circle on a daily route, was a certified flight instructor. He was working for a company called Air North based out of Fairbanks. The main charters out of Circle City were for trips across the Arctic Circle where the passengers received a certificate for the achievement. I still had my airplane in Fairbanks and wanted to get it up to Circle. I had already received my Student Pilot License and passed my ground school. I started flying lessons in Fairbanks and soon I had built up a few flight hours. Gordon, on one of his very few slow days, came down to Fairbanks and flew the airplane to Circle. Once the plane was in Circle, I was able to fly with Tim in the evenings. After a short time, he told me I could solo the aircraft.

Not wanting to make my first landing on an airstrip, I flew the aircraft across the Yukon River and landed on a gravel bar across from Circle. I shut down the aircraft, got out and walked around on the gravel bar and waved at all the folks watching from the village across the river. I really thought I was being cool. It was all great until I went to start the airplane to fly back over to Circle. I put large rocks under the wheels and set the brake on the aircraft. I positioned the propeller, turned on the magnetos and pulled the propeller through. The engine wouldn't start. I tried several times without success. I decided to set the throttle up a little higher. Tried once more without success. Increased the throttle a little more. This time the engine started and the plane skipped over the rocks and started to take off without me. I was able to grab the strut and swing myself into the cockpit. The door flew closed from the propeller wash hitting me on the ear. I was still able to reach the throttle and close it off enough to stop the aircraft. All this was happening with an audience along the river bank in Circle City. Fortunately, I was on the opposite side of the aircraft so they could not see me going through all the gyrations. I got into the aircraft with my bleeding ear and took off returning to the Circle airstrip a little smarter than when I left. No one really figured out how close I came to losing the aircraft. It did take a few weeks for me to get the courage to fly again. I blamed it on how busy we were working on helicopters and doing flying jobs.

Early in the season, I talked Gordon into loaning me a helicopter and a pilot. My plan was to take a couple of weeks off, fly up to the homestead site and build a cabin. Robert (Fred) Friedrich and Dusan Kovak went with me. Fred was the pilot and Dusan was a builder. We loaded up the helicopter with chainsaws, fuel, tools to build with and a chainsaw wench. We arrived in mid- May. Fred was only able to stay for a couple of days before returning to work back at Sunshine Helicopters. Dusan and I went right to work preparing the land. We were able to cut down trees and remove the limbs, dig holes down to the river gravel to place posts to support the floor and the walls. We laid down the first row of logs and decided they were too heavy to handle that way, so we stood the rest up like a fence. Once we had the walls up we were able to wench the top cap logs up onto the walls. We then built the end gables using a drill and re-bar to hold everything in place. The last thing we did was place the ridgepole and purlins in place on the gable ends.

While we were there, the weather was pretty good so one night Dusan and I decided to take a hike up the valley. We heard some noise that sounded like people up the valley from where we were. It was only about two miles up the river to the next cabin which was built by a couple of guys who were still staying there at the time. Their cabin was built on the bluff that I had been fishing from when I discovered the first claim jar nailed to the tree. They were surprised to see us come walking up to the front door, but very glad to meet us. We spent a few hours with them and enjoyed our conversation. They were happy to talk to someone new in the valley. When we left their cabin, we realized it was getting dark and we still had quite a distance to hike. As we were hiking back down the valley toward our camp, I got the strange feeling that we were being followed. I asked Dusan if he felt anything, and he responded that he was glad it wasn't just him who had that feeling. We made it back to camp without any problems but the feeling would not go away. We finally climbed into bed and Dusan went right to sleep. Dusan could snore louder than a bear, and that might have been what saved us that night. Even though we had the rifles right next to us, I had a lot of trouble going to sleep. Every little noise from outside our tent would awaken me. The next morning when we finally climbed out of our tent and looked around our camp, we noticed that the ground was all torn up about 50 feet out from our tent. There were also claw marks ripped down the sides of several trees. I guess we had been followed the night before by a very angry bear. I realized then that in this valley, we were not alone. In fact, the valley was home to many bears.

The bears never bothered us during the day while we were working on building the cabin. I figured the noise was what kept them away. After that one night of terror, both Dusan and I slept with one eye open and one hand on a gun. We had to leave earlier then we hoped due to the workload back home in Circle City. Still, the sight of the helicopter's return was a very welcome event. Gordon needed me back at the hangar and so away we went. I was a bit disappointed at the time, because I had failed to finish the cabin and I was not sure when I would be able to return to complete the task. As it turned out, I would not return until I was ready to live there.

Later in 1976, I came home to Fairbanks after an extended stay in Circle City to find that my wife had left me. My two children were left behind and suddenly I found myself as a single parent. Michael, my youngest, was only one year old and still in diapers. Fred, my oldest, was three and completely clueless as to what had happened to Mom. After finding the kids at home, I took them over to their grandmother's house for a few days while I tried to get my life back together. I was able to rent a cabin from George O'Leary, a relative of the family, located in

Circle City. The cabin was in need of a new roof and some other work but in trade for some rent I rushed back up to Circle City and proceeded to put on a new roof and fix up the cabin as best I could. I then returned to Fairbanks and picked up the kids from their grandmother's house and returned with them to Circle. More and more it looked like keeping the Brooks Range homestead was going to be impossible.

In May of 1977, the town of Circle flooded. During spring break-up, the ice in the Yukon River usually grumbles, growls, crunches, and crashes as the ice flows out. It is one of the most amazing sights anyone can experience. During this spring break-up, an ice dam formed downstream from Circle City. Most the time the river will rise a few feet and the ice dam will let go and the river will move on. This year that was not the case. Instead, the river started going up at the bank about three o'clock in the afternoon. One of the old timers was standing next to me watching the river level go up. He had lived in Circle for several years and he told me not to worry because the ice would go out before the river ever went over its banks in Circle. The water level was coming up quite fast. I decided I would return to my cabin and start putting things up in my loft. I had only been at the cabin about 20 minutes when the neighbor who lived on the river came over in a panic asking for my help. I rushed over to their cabin and helped get the older folks out and into my truck to get them to higher ground. The water was already over the banks and up against their cabin. The water was still coming up very fast. After helping them, I tried to get back to my cabin but the water had already beat me there. My cabin sat in a low hollow and the water hit it from all sides. I realized it was a lost cause. I rushed over to the hangar and started putting things up on higher shelves. It wasn't long before the hangar was surrounded by water. Soon the water was coming in through the bottom plate of the hangar wall. There was so much pressure hitting the wall that the water was spraying in like a wide spray nozzle and the water was reaching out about eight feet onto the hangar floor. I knew then we were in a lot of trouble.

I pushed out our Hughes 500C helicopter which I had just finished putting back together the day before in preparation for the summer season. I jumped in, started it up and about that time Gordon showed up. I jumped out and went to work on the old Hiller 12D helicopter that was setting outside. It had not been started since we had parked it the fall before. I found a battery in the back room. By now I was wading in water up to my knees. I will say it was very, very cold water. I waded out to the Hiller and slammed in the battery. I didn't have time to bolt it down. I pulled off the covers and the tie downs. By now the water was up to the belly of the helicopter. I climbed in and hit the starter. The engine cranked hard but finally caught and started up. I was about to fly it out of the water when Gordon came wading back to pick that one up. I went back into the hangar and picked up more stuff until my legs were so numb I could hardly walk.

By now the water reached the Trading Post. I made my way over there to find people in the basement. They were trying to save the food and the booze which was stored in the basement. Water was rushing in and people had formed a chain. They were passing things up the stairs as fast as they could. The town preacher showed up and asked if she could help. Someone handed her a case of whiskey. She almost had a heart attack right there! She turned and ran away.

The river stopped its rise about nine o'clock in the evening. I guess the major ice dam finally let go. In the end, the river came up about 10 feet. It would have been more except the river formed a levee on its own. The ice built up along the bank of the river. I went over the next morning and climbed up on the ice levee and looked over into the river. It was still higher than the bank but the levee was holding it back. That year, several cabins lost their front porches and front yards. Several dogs drowned because people could not get to them in time. One man had his whole pickup loaded with his belongings and was making a run for it but never made it. The river took his pickup away and only by the grace of God was he saved. That was the same old timer who told me the river would not go over its banks.

The hangar had a water line about four feet up on the walls. I was able to save most all of the more expensive items in the hangar. The 1,000-gallon fuel tank, which was setting on the same pad as the Hiller helicopter, was gone. In its place was a block of ice the size of a small cabin. My old Chevy Nova went completely under water. It took me awhile to get it running again. My cabin looked like a bomb had gone off on the inside. All the furniture was in the middle of the room. The kids' beds were ruined along with all their bedding. We all lost a lot of our belongings that year. The Red Cross showed up and were a great help to everyone in the village. They helped me get new beds and bedding for the kids. The large ice chunks were laying all over town like great monoliths from another world and lasted for most of the month of May before they all melted away.

Sunshine Copters was very lucky. We saved the helicopters and most of the very expensive tools. I was able to save most of the new parts in the parts rooms and the aircraft manuals were all up on high shelves. The water reached the very edge of our work tables in the office but did not go over the top. I was able to save my pickup truck. Gordon was able to save the Trading Post. The basement flooded, but the main floor was spared. Living along the very powerful Yukon River can be very risky. They told us it was a 100-year flood. Since that flood, there have been several more. The Yukon River goes where it wants.

During the summer of 1977, I made several trips into town to get aircraft parts and supplies. On one of my last trips into town in late September on my way back up to Circle City, I came across two ladies hitchhiking on the road. The road to Circle is a lonely road going only one way in or out. I stopped and asked them if they wanted a lift. At first they were not sure if I was a good guy or a sex starved Alaskan looking for a good time. I assured them that I was on a parts run for my helicopter company and could take them all the way to the Yukon River. To me they both looked like they could take care of themselves quite well.

One of the two girls was Mary Anderson. It seemed that we both hit it off right away. I was going through a tough time and shared with Mary some of the things going on. I told her I was still married, but without a wife. When we got up to Circle City that evening the sun was still shining and several other people had arrived. One group of guys brought guitars and with little coaxing a party just started out of nothing. This was pretty normal for folks out in the bush. Mary and her friend came over and several other people joined in the party. Talking to Mary really felt good and we stayed up almost all night listening to music and telling stories about our many dreams.

When I told Mary I had an airplane she asked if I would take her for a ride. I told her I had just soloed not too long before but she didn't seem to care. I realized she was a gutsy lady. The next morning, I met her at the plane. She was dressed in a leather jacket with a leather flying cap. If she had had goggles she would have looked like a World War One flying ace. I laughed and I laughed, boy did that feel good. We got into the plane and we took off flying over Circle City and then on over to Central. We landed in Central, walked around a while and then we flew back to Circle. It was a short trip but a great time for both of us. It gave me hope that I could live again. When we got back to Circle, Mary was so excited that she ran to tell her girlfriend all the details of the flight. They only stayed in Circle for a couple of days, but before she left I asked for her address. She was from Rochester, Minnesota -- long way from home. We said our tearful goodbyes but somehow I knew this girl was going to be an important part of my life.

As summer waned into winter, I continued to work on the helicopters, raise my two boys and keep my life together. It seemed to me to be a very cold winter. The divorce was final in December 1977 and I was granted full custody of the two boys. I still had the house in Fairbanks, but was attempting to sell it. I would take the boys from Circle into town on weekends as long as the road was open. We would visit their grandmother and stay at the house in Fairbanks. It was a pretty empty home. The kids were still too young for school, so they would hang out with me at the hangar and even helped me build the other Hiller that Gordon bought at the auction in Arizona. In the winter, things at the company would slow down or even come to a complete stop. This gave us lots of time to work on other projects. I was realizing that 1978 would be the last year I had to keep the homestead and the cabin. As the winter darkened so did my depression. If it had not been for the kids, who were the sunshine and joy in my life, and the letters I received from Mary, I'm not sure how I would have made it.

10

TRAPPERS AND DOGS

During the Spring of 1975 a man wandered into Circle City named Marvin. He had come to Alaska with two other friends. Their background was a bit shady and were most likely hiding out from the law. They must have thought they could hide out in the Alaska wilderness. They made the attempt, but between the bears and the mosquitoes, Marvin's two friends left him and went back to the Lower 48. When Marvin arrived in Circle he was in pretty bad shape. He was half starved, dirty and very tired. We nicknamed him Starvin' Marvin. Gordon gave him a room and food and hired him to help out around the Trading Post. He worked there through the summer and winter of 1975-1976. He was a very hard worker and Gordon supported him during his stay.

In the Fall of 1976, Marvin wanted to try his hand at trapping and building a wilderness cabin. Gordon took him up in the helicopter and flew him out into the wilderness and they found an area that looked suitable for a cabin and trap line.

They came back to Circle and Marvin bought supplies, traps
and a rifle. He also had a black lab dog named Jake. Once he
was all ready to go, Gordon flew him and Jake out to the area
and turned them loose to do their thing. Gordon would fly out
once a month to check on Marvin and resupply him. I would
go with Gordon on days that were slow at the hangar. The first
few trips we were amazed at what a nice cabin Marvin had built
with his bare hands. He had come out of Montana and had
worked as a logger so his skills with a chainsaw and an ax were
apparent in the construction of his cabin.

Around February of 1977 on one of those trips out to
Marvin's cabin for resupply, I was with Gordon. We arrived at
his cabin with one of the helicopters. The noise was extreme
and we were sure that Marvin heard us landing. After we shut
the aircraft down, I noticed that Jake was leaning against a tree
covered in snow. We could tell he was dead and frozen stiff.
We got out of the helicopter and began to unload the supplies
and take them over to the cabin. The door was unlocked and
the cabin was warm inside so we knew Marvin was around. It
wasn't long before we heard Marvin hollering out in the woods
that he was coming. He finally got there with his back pack and
snow shoes on his back. He was pretty winded from running
through the snow. Marvin was beyond happy to see us. We all
went into the cabin where he fixed us some coffee and told us
all about his trapping adventures. He had been doing quite well
with the trapping and had many furs hanging on his cabin wall.
Mostly martin, a few mink and a couple of beaver.

We finally got around to asking him about Jake. In a sor-
rowful tone, he explained that the last trip when Gordon had

delivered his supplies, there was a frozen chicken in the box. Marvin was really looking forward to frying up that chicken. On the day he decided to cook the chicken he put it out on his table to thaw, then he took Jake and his backpack and headed out to check traps. Somewhere along the way, Jake took off on his own. Marvin didn't think much about that as Jake often took off after rabbits or other creatures but would always rejoin him on the trap line. This time, however, Jake went back to the cabin and pushed open the front door, went inside and ate Marvin's chicken. When Marvin returned that afternoon cold and hungry, looking forward to cooking up the chicken, what he found really angered him; there was Jake under the table still licking his chops and looking quite satisfied with what he had done. The cabin was cold due to the open door. Marvin not being the forgiving type, pulled out the rifle and shot and killed Jake. He told us that the next morning he realized what he had done and was feeling very remorseful. He had laid Jake in the snow the night before and now Jake was frozen stiff. He felt so bad about the whole thing that he decided to lean Jake against a tree so he could see him out the window and remind himself what he had done.

Once spring was over and summer was fast approaching, Marvin returned to Circle and worked for Gordon during the summer of 1977. In the Fall of 1977, I asked Marvin if he would be willing to go out to my homestead and finish my cabin. I knew the following summer was the last chance I had to save the homestead. I also knew that if I went out there, the kids would be with me and I needed a finished cabin. Marvin agreed to go to finish my cabin and said he would stay there through the winter and come back in the spring of 1978. I paid him up front and Gordon flew him out to the cabin. My mistake was paying him up front.

Around the same time as the Marvin adventures, I had two dogs. One was a malamute husky named Moose and the other a small springer spaniel named Cricket. I raised Moose from a puppy and Moose had become a bit famous in Circle City. He was kind of a quirky pup and I remember he could eat a tremendous amount of food. One evening when Moose was still a small puppy, I had some friends over. We were all drinking beer when I remarked that Moose would eat a large coffee can of food if I gave it to him. That got everyone to start betting he couldn't do it. I took the five-dollar bet and filled a coffee can full of dog kibble and put the can down for Moose to eat. He dove right in and started chowing down on the food. Soon you could tell he was getting full but he wouldn't stop eating. It took him awhile but he ate everything in the can. He was so full that he could hardly walk. I could see he was in stress so I let him outside. He would waddle a short distance, let go with a tremendous fart, then walk a little further and do the same thing. This went on for quite a while before he was back to his old self. Needless to say, it cured him from hogging food again. We all got a good laugh out of this at Moose's expense, and I got my five dollars.

As Moose was growing up, and during the stage where he should have lost his puppy fur, shedding became very erratic and his fur became splotchy. We couldn't figure what was wrong with him, so I took him to the vet. The veterinarian suggested that all his fur be shaved off and he believed that

Moose's fur would grow back normal. So, at his suggestion, that's what happened. When we got Moose back from getting shaved, he looked like a long legged, spotted pig. We could not help but laugh. Everyone who saw him would start laughing at him and I believe that was when he decided he didn't like humans. Between the food incident and getting shaved, it was just too much for him. Don't get me wrong, Moose would not bite anyone, he was way too smart for that. Moose found other ways to get even with people.

When I moved up to Circle City to help run the helicopter business, I took both Moose and Cricket with me. Cricket was a great hunting dog with tremendous smarts. He was super easy to train and was always eager to please. Between him and Moose, I believe Cricket was the Alpha dog. Moose was three times bigger and believed in his own mind that he controlled everything, but Cricket just knew how to get around and Moose would follow him everywhere. Moose wasn't much into chasing other animals, but Cricket was a hunter and loved chasing rabbits, usually right between your legs. He would really look disappointed if you failed to shoot whatever he chased to you.

In Circle City, many people had sled dogs and trap lines. One thing that would get a dog killed faster than anything was getting caught chasing down someone's trap line. Well Cricket wasn't quite up on those rules and he made the mistake of getting caught in a snare trap, I'm sure while chasing a rabbit. Fortunately for him, I was walking outside the hangar that day and barely heard his distinct way of howling. I recognized his howl, so I took off into the woods and went toward the noise finally finding him curled up in a ball crying like a baby. The good news was the snare had not damaged his leg and the trapper had not yet come down the line. As it was, the trapper knew it was Cricket who had been around his trap line and he warned me never to let that happen again or I would have a dead dog on my hands. On that adventure, I was able to save Cricket.

Later on, I took both the dogs with me to Fairbanks back to the house I still owned. We were only there for a couple of days, but when I came home one evening after being in town, I found Moose with a bullet hole in his jaw and one in his shoulder. Cricket never returned. I can only assume they got into someone's yard and both were shot. Cricket was killed, but Moose recovered from his wounds and went on to have more adventures.

I took Moose back up to Circle City with me after he recovered from his wounds. I know I mentioned Moose's dislike for people. Moose's fur, after the shaving incident, never did grow back like it was supposed to. He had fur on his back, face and legs. He also had a beautiful tail. There were only splotches of fur on his sides and belly. Of course, this made him a very unusual looking malamute. Most of his life was spent in Circle City and due to the tourist industry, he became a bit of a celebrity. Tourists were attracted to Circle City because, at the time, it was the farthest North one could drive. I called it the end of I-5 where the road ended at the banks of the Yukon River. The Yukon River is the 5th largest river in the world. Where the Yukon River goes past Circle City, it is approximately two miles wide. During breakup in the spring, it is really a sight to see with

the ice grinding along, piling up along the banks, and the tremendous noise it makes. It has always been an amazing annual
event. The river flows along at six to nine miles per hour and
with all the silt in the river, it makes a constant swishing sound
as it slides past the river banks. I might add that since the oil
pipeline has been built and the Dalton Highway exists, one can
drive all the way to the Arctic Ocean. Consequently, Circle City
has lost a lot of its appeal.

Moose would hang out on the porch of the Yukon Trading
Post. The sun would shine there and he liked lying in the sun...
no fur and all. Because of his missing fur and unusual looks,
he became a bit of an attraction and not always in a good way.
Many times, I would see a tourist's camera in their hand taking
pictures of Moose. Of course, they gave him a wide birth due
to his unique looks. I am sure they must have thought he had
mange or some other disease.

Moose was a very curious and attentive dog and anything
out of the ordinary would catch his eye and he would go to investigate. When it came to tourists, it would usually be the dogs
they brought with them that piqued Moose's interest. He would
spot a poodle or some other interesting dog and away he would
go down to the tourist's parking area to check it out. I would
hear a commotion down by the river landing and there would
be Moose trying to check out these other dogs. Of course,
the people didn't like that, thinking Moose had the mange and
would start chasing him off with sticks and rocks. Moose would
trot back up to the Trading Post and lie back down like he didn't
have a care in the world. But not so! He would wait for those
same people to come up to the Trading Post and once inside,

he would get up, stretch, and wander back down to the camp-ing area and proceed to pee on any of their gear that was left outside. Usually it would be their packs, tents or chairs. Once accomplishing the task, he would return to the trading post and lie back down like nothing had happened. I witnessed this many times throughout the summer months and I could never break him of that habit.

Once in a while, I would be heading over to the Trading Post and Moose would see me coming. He would jump up and with a snarl and a terrible sounding growl, he would attack me, knocking me off my feet. He would proceed to act like he was killing me. We would roll around on the ground tussling with each other putting on quite a show for the tourists. He would be growling and snarling the whole time but would never hurt me. Once satisfied that the show had accomplished what he wanted, he would get up, shake himself off, wag his tail at me and go back over and lie down. It was all play for both of us, but to the tourists it looked very real.

Moose actually lived in the hangar where I worked on the helicopters. He spent a lot of time lying in front of the heater and sleeping during the cold winter months. He had a habit of keeping one eye open and would watch me working on the helicopters. He would wait until I was in some terrible position when I was unable to get up or out in a hurry. He would then get up, yawn, walk over to where I was working and deliber-ately fart some terrible stinky gas that would make my eyes wa-ter. Once accomplished and with me cussing him out he would wag his tail and go back over to the heater and lie back down. Moose hated people.

Moose was not without his talents. He had a fixation for Fig Newton cookies and could catch one from several feet away. He never missed. The hangar was 50 feet deep and you could throw a cookie the length of the hangar and he would catch it. One night I made the mistake of leaving a new package of Fig Newton cookies on top of a cabinet that held all our expensive instruments for the helicopters. When I arrived the next morning to feed our illustrious guard dog, to my surprise I found an empty bag of Fig Newton cookies and a lot of very expensive instruments laying on the concrete floor. To say the least, Gordon was not a happy person and flat laid down the law that Moose could not stay in the hangar by himself.

Moose also took a disliking to the owner of the Trading Post. Gordon had not purchased the Trading Post yet and at that time Frank Warren still owned it. Every Thursday the plane from Fairbanks would arrive with the Trading Post supplies. It was always a rush to get the supplies unloaded so the plane could take off on time. Frank would run the supplies up to the Trading Post in his pickup. He would pile some of the supplies at the back door of the Trading Post when he had other things to do. As soon as he would leave the supplies alone, Moose would run over and pee on them. Of course, this was not acceptable and Frank would grab his rifle and chase after Moose. I could always tell when Moose was in trouble because he would hit the hangar door really hard, and if it opened he would run passed me like his tail was on fire and bury himself back in the parts room under the boxes. If the door did not open, I would run over, open the door and he would almost knock me over. He would always leave me to ward off Frank with his rifle dead set on shooting Moose. I could always tell when Moose was in real trouble because of the speed and look on his face when he would run to me to hide. I think after the first shooting, he knew what a rifle looked like and wanted nothing to do with them.

The first winter that Moose had to stay outside of the hangar, I realized he would freeze to death without somewhere warm to go. I decided I would build him a dog house on the side of the hangar. I insulated the house and ducted the paint room exhaust fan into his dog house. I put a thick blanket over his door so he could get in and out when he wanted. The dog house stayed warm throughout the winter. There was one small problem: if we forgot to get him out of his dog house before we started painting something, he would come flying out of there choking and coughing with a very angry look on his face. Moose hated people.

Moose did have a girlfriend. There were very few loose dogs in Circle and the ones who were loose had to behave themselves or they would end up on a chain or dead. Moose's girlfriend was an Irish Setter named Madeleine. She was a very pretty dog for a village dog and she took to Moose's heated dog house during the winter. That first winter that Moose was outside in his new heated dog house, Madeleine just moved right in with him. I went out one morning to feed Moose and there she was. Moose looked pretty satisfied with himself, so I just let it go. I figured it was his business and he seemed very happy with the arrangements so I just let it be. Moose would never share his dog food with anyone except Madeleine. I had to increase the food allotment for the two of them.

Moose, besides hating people, hated ravens. Ravens are very intelligent birds and very opportunistic. Moose was on a chain during the summer because he would not behave himself. I would feed him in the morning, taking his dog food and putting it close to his house. As soon as I left, the ravens would attack. Now Moose was easily out-maneuvered by these birds. One would land on his dog house and the other raven would stand just outside his reach. Moose would run to the end of his chain to get the one outside his circle and the other bird would jump down and take some of his food. The ravens would do this back and forth stealing as much food as they could get away with. One day they were using the same method when Moose's chain came out of his dog house. What a surprise for the raven just outside of his circle. He expected Moose to stop but not this time. Pow! Moose caught his first and only raven. He had a lot of pent up frustration from all the weeks of chasing those birds and once he caught one raven, he just tore it to shreds and ate it. He pranced around all day out there so proud of himself. This was the last time the ravens stole Moose's food.

There was one other time Moose broke his chain. Moose weighed 135lb and was very strong in the neck and shoulders. I had him on a very strong chain but with him pulling on it all the time he was able to break the ring holding it to the dog house. I was inside the hangar working on a helicopter during the middle of summer and the hangar doors were open. I was unaware that Moose had gotten loose. It wasn't until I got a call from the far side of town yelling at me that Moose was harassing this man's dog team. He said he would shoot him if I did not get down there and get Moose out of his yard. I jumped in my truck and drove down to the end of town and found Moose all tangled up around a wooden stake. I untangled him then told him to get back home. He did mind me most of the time so he headed back down to the hangar dragging his chain as I was following him in my pickup. Just about a block from the hangar, Moose cut across in front of me. The chain got caught under the right front tire and pulled him under the left front tire and I ran over him. I heard him yelp and I felt the bump. I got out and ran to him. He was lying there crying like a baby and I thought I had really hurt him badly. About that time, some of the other loose dogs in town heard him crying and they ran over and attacked him. I guess they figured he was down so they could take advantage of it and settle all their old grudges they had with him. What a recovery Moose had! It was like he had never been hurt. He jumped up and even with the chain still under the other tire, he tore the other dogs up. It only took him a split second to win the fight with three other dogs. Moose was amazing. There he stood with his legs apart and tail up in the air and when he looked at me, I could tell he was still pissed at me for running over him. Fortunately for me, he got over it. But Moose still hated people.

One afternoon in the fall I was headed up to the Trading Post restaurant to eat my dinner and I noticed a new truck in town. It had a flat bed with what looked to be a 10-foot high cage on the back. Inside the cage was a very pretty female malamute in heat. At the time, Moose was still running around loose. Usually when I went up to the Trading Post to eat, Moose would typically just go up to the porch on the Trading Post, lie down and wait for me. I had gone into the restaurant and was already eating when a friend came in and whispered in my ear that Moose was in the cage with the female and actually hooked up with her. I looked outside through the back door and sure enough, there was Moose all hooked up with the female. I looked at the cage and could not figure how Moose had gotten in there. I knew that if the owner found out this mangy looking dog had gotten to his prize female, he would most likely shoot him.

I went back in the restaurant and struck up a conversation with the owner of the truck. I kept him busy as long as I could. He finally said he needed to get going after he went to the bathroom. When he went into the bathroom I went out the back door and yelled at Moose to get out of the cage immediately. He must have known that trouble was on the way, because he jumped up on the fence clawing his way up and over the top and ran back toward the hangar just as the man came out the back door. The man never knew what had happened. He gave me a wave and drove down by the river where he had a boat waiting for him. He loaded all the dogs and his supplies in the boat, parked his truck and across the river he went. He had told me that his plan was to camp a few days across the river before heading on down river. I figured that was that and all was good.

Well, I figured wrong...the problem was Moose had fallen in love with that female sled dog. Later in the evening I couldn't find Moose around the hangar so I went looking for him. I found him down by the river bank. He was howling and moaning like a forlorn baby. He would howl a loud cry and I could hear the female howl back to him. It seemed that the feeling was mutual. Madeleine would sleep with any other dog so I guess it was only lust that kept the two of them together.

Like I said before, the Yukon River is two miles across with a six to nine mile current. Did I mention how cold and silty the water is? I figured Moose would just have to say his goodbyes and give it up so I was surprised beyond belief when Moose suddenly jumped into the river and began to swim across. I had never seen Moose get into any water before this and I didn't think he could even swim. The problem was the strength of the current and as I watched and yelled for him to come back he was being dragged down the river farther and farther away from Circle and as well as his destination. I watched with concern as Moose went around the bend about a mile down river from Circle. It looked to me like he may have made it one third of the way across before he disappeared. I really figured this would be the end of Moose. He would get too tired and cold to get back to either shore and he would drown in the silty river and I would never know because his body would sink out of sight or be swept all the way down to the Arctic Ocean.

I went home that night with a very heavy heart knowing that I had just lost my best worst friend. The next morning, I woke up in my cabin without Moose. I was fixing breakfast on the stove when off in the distance I heard that same mournful howl I had heard the night before. I ran down to the river and there was Moose howling out his broken heart. He looked pretty tired, so I got his bowl of food and brought it down to him. Usually he dove right in and ate his food in a hurry. This time, he didn't eat for three days, he just sat by the river waiting for her return. Moose finally gave up, came home and started eating again. But he just didn't have the same spark in his eyes after that, well, until Madeline showed back up.

11

THE TRIP BEGINS

Throughout the winter I had been making lists upon lists of what we would need at the cabin. Mary and I had been writing back and forth all winter and I asked her sometime during January 1978 if she would be willing to go with me. I told her my kids were going, but her parents were very worried about her going out into the unknown wilderness. I wrote her parents a letter and told them I had a lot of resources and would not be taking my two kids with me if I thought anything would happen to them. I guess that must have convinced them because Mary wrote back and said she would go with us. The date we set for leaving from Fairbanks to the homestead property was April 17, 1978 which would give me a few days to spare on the five-month requirement to keep the homestead patent. I put together a long list of required items for the trip and by the time Mary arrived in Fairbanks, I had most all of the stuff we would need to survive five months at the cabin. I assured Mary the cabin was habitable and ready to go. Marvin would have completed the building by the time we arrived.

The day Mary arrived in Fairbanks, I left the kids in Circle City with friends and I drove into town and picked her up at the train station. It was getting late when she arrived so we went out to my house that I still owned but was in the process of selling. The next morning, we drove back to Circle City, picked up the rest of our supplies along with Moose and my two kids. We stayed at the house for a couple of days and during that stay, Moose disappeared. I can only think that he got into someone's property and was shot. I was really looking forward to taking him with us if for no other reason than to be a bear dog. I took three guns with me; a Ruger .41, a Savage 300 and Gordon's double barreled 12 gauge shot gun. By the time we were ready to go, we filled my pickup truck with our gear which came to around 1,000 pounds counting Mary, the kids and myself and that was a full load for the Howard aircraft we would be leaving in.

We drove down to the small airstrip in Fairbanks around nine o'clock in the morning where we met up with Don Taylor, the pilot who would be flying us up to the cabin. We were all very excited to be going, well, maybe not the kids so much. We all pitched in and loaded the aircraft, tied everything down and then we all climbed in. There were several people who had come down to see us off. As the aircraft powered up, we waved our goodbyes and the plane started rolling down the runway. I knew within moments that we were in trouble. It was supposed to be about a four-hour flight to the cabin but it ended up being about 45 seconds. As luck would have it, the plane didn't catch fire and the ice pond didn't break through. No one was hurt except for my bloody nose. We missed all the airplanes on the side of the runway by inches and if the fuel tank had not been there we might have gotten in the air higher and crashed into the dirt bank on the other side -- that might have killed us. Anyway, I look back on it and we were very lucky all the way around. Even if the flight had been successful, landing anywhere near the cabin might not have been possible. I can't imagine how we would have walked all that gear and supplies into the cabin. When we did arrive there, the snow was deep and I didn't see any gravel bars that Don could have landed on.

After the crash, it took Mary and me a couple of days to regroup. We were both a little shaken up, but I told Mary the best thing to do was get back in another airplane and press on before fear took hold of us for good. I gathered up most of the money I had left and chartered a local flying service to take us into the cabin. They were flying Helio Courier aircraft, a great little plane that could handle all our gear and the four of us without any issues. These planes are work horses that can land on short strips and get off just as fast. They can also fly very slow but they get you there in one piece.

We were scheduled to leave at 10:00 am on the 19th of April. As luck would have it, after loading the airplane and taxiing out towards the runway, we were stopped by the Federal Aviation Administration (FAA) and the National Transportation Safety Board (NTSB). Seems they had some questions for me about the crash we had been in a couple of days before. I was really hoping to get away before they caught up to me. I knew I would end up putting Don Taylor in a terrible spot. We delayed the flight for a couple of hours while I went over to the FAA building and gave them a statement on what happened. Seems like we were overweight, didn't have a proper emergency locator beacon on board and not enough seat belts for the number of passengers. They came down pretty hard on Don. Not only did he lose his airplane, but they took away his pilot's license. After that incident, he never wanted to talk to me again, and I really couldn't blame him. I know I felt terrible about what happened. The FAA Inspector gave me a good thrashing, saying I should have known better and if anything like that happened again in the future I would lose my Airframe & Powerplant license as well as my Inspection Authorization certificate.

They finally let me go and I returned to Mary and the kids. We were very close to missing the flight out, but we ended up leaving around two o'clock and we still had a long three-hour flight ahead of us. Luckily the flight was uneventful and the weather was sunny and clear all the way. After all the bad luck we seemed to be having we were finally going to get there. We set down along the Ambler River about 400 yards from the cabin. It was almost five o'clock, but we still had plenty of daylight left. The snow was fairly deep and the plane stopped rather quickly. We off loaded all our gear into the snow, stomped down an area of snow in front of the aircraft so he could get a start and once he was ready, he gave it the power and in short order was in the air and going away.

I remember the noise of the engine as he took off and disappeared over the mountains and then came the quiet. The stillness of where we were became deafening. We found ourselves whispering before we realized we were the only humans for miles around. There we stood up to our knees in snow with the sun burning down on us giving us enough heat to get past the freezing point. All our supplies were piled in the snow right next to us and it looked big. The cabin seemed a long way off. We could see it about a quarter mile away. Michael broke the silence when he asked if he could go back to his grandmother's house. I told him "not today, we will be staying here for a while". Soon he started crying and then Fred started crying as well. I told them we really needed to get busy and haul all our stuff over to the cabin. Mary picked up Michael and I grabbed some gear and we started trudging through the snow and over to the cabin.

My first close up view of the cabin gave me a bit of a shock. Marvin had vacated the cabin long before it was completed. When we sent Marvin up to the homestead to finish the cabin, I sent with him a small wood stove and chimney pipe. He had cut the top and bottom out of a five gallon can large enough to fit a six-inch stove pipe through the middle. That was his poor man's insulated pipe going through the roof. He had installed the stove and pipe through the roof.

Before Marvin left, he had installed all the roof rafters and covered the roof with Griffolyn plastic to make a roof now covered in deep snow. Thank God he had installed the stove and pipe through the roof. Still there was no floor, just the floor joists were installed. The cabin door was not installed and was built laying on the floor joists. I guess it had become too cold for him to survive the fall months and he left once he ran out of wood. The cabin had no windows cut out so it was cold and dark inside. By the time we gathered everything over to the cabin it was getting dark, and the cold temperature was settling in. I realized that getting through the first night was going to be a real challenge. The kids were hungry and tired and the look on Mary's face said it all. We were in trouble and the only way out was to dig down deep and make it happen.

I found some dry wood and started a fire in the wood stove. Mary dug out some peanut butter and cheese. We also had bread and crackers so that became our first meal. Fred and Michael were crying and wanted to go home. I figured that once we had some food in us and a fire to get warm by, we would survive that first night. We dug out our sleeping bags and put them on the door laying across the floor joists. This is where we spent the night in 12 degree temperatures. Mary was on one side of the door and I was on the other side with the two kids between us. It wasn't the best night of sleep, but we were very tired from the long day, so made the best of it.

I was up early the next morning as soon as any daylight was showing. I went right to work shoveling trails around the cabin and getting the chainsaw up and running. The first job was getting trees cut down to make floor boards. I would cut down a tree, limb it, cut it to about 12 foot in length and drag it near the cabin. I got several trees cut down that morning and piled them near the cabin. I also found more dry wood and got another fire going in the stove. Mary went to work putting together a breakfast for the kids and sorting through the supplies. I began cutting free hand long slabs off of the trees that I had near the cabin. Each slab was about 1 to 1 1/2 inches thick and 8 to 10 inches wide. Once I had several slabs cut, I would lay them down flat and run the chain saw down the edges between the slabs until they fit together. The morning temperature was pretty cold but once we were moving around it became tolerable.

I was really feeling bad for Mary who had put all her trust in me. I could tell she was worried to the bone, but not once did she complain about things that should have been. She just dove in and worked right alongside of me. By the end of the first day, I had cut enough planks to cover a large area of the floor. We brought Visqueen with us and I had put that down on the floor joists first then put the planks down next. At least by the second night we were able to spread out a little bit, but it was still too cold to sleep apart. On the second morning, I continued cutting floor boards. I also hung the front door with Mary's help so we could hold the heat in the cabin better. It took me about four days of using the chainsaw to cut the logs before I had enough to cover the whole floor.

I brought nails with us so once all the boards were cut, I began fitting them onto the floor joists and nailing them down. Keeping the chainsaw sharp was a nightly job. I brought several wooden boxes of five gallon cans of gasoline and chainsaw oil. I spent a lot of time holding that Homelite 350 chainsaw. I also brought a McCulloch 10-10 chainsaw as a back-up. They were by far the most important tools I used. The days were full, I got a lot accomplished and I must admit I had no trouble sleeping at night.

Once the floor was installed, I had to reinstall the wood stove. I brought a granny oven which mounted into the six-inch stovepipe right above the woodstove. We also had a large teapot that we left on the stove with water always hot and ready to use. I think it was about the seventh day we realized we just might make it after all. The weather remained sunny and each day was getting warmer. Snow was actually melting off the roof. The river was still iced over but we could see open water around the edges.

The roof became our next job. I climbed up on the roof and very carefully removed the snow off the plastic. We brought two white plastic five gallon buckets with us. With the help of the kids and Mary, we began filling the buckets with dirt. Since the ground was frozen it was very difficult to find dirt. With each passing day, the dirt bank in front of the cabin that faced south began to melt more and more. We were able to dig into the bank and get enough dirt to cover the roof to almost five inches thick.

By the time we had the dirt on the roof, which took several days, the snow around the trees was melted. This exposed the thick moss which grows in that part of the forest. We would go on moss hunting trips with the kids, filling the buckets up with as much moss as they could hold. This took us several days and then a few weeks to finish covering the roof with dirt and moss. Those white five gallon buckets were the most used item in our camp. We hauled water, dirt, moss, laundry and anything else we needed to carry. We had a third bucket with a toilet seat mounted on it for our early bathroom. Eventually I was able to build an actual outhouse.

In the first load of supplies, I had brought most of the immediate things that Mary, the kids and I would need such as food, paper products, utensils, pots and pans, a radio, bedding, clothes, work gear, the buckets and necessary tools. Gordon arranged to have another load of supplies brought out to us after we had been there about 30 days. That load contained more Griffolyn sheathing, cabin windows, a small Honda generator, sheet metal, food, rope, foam bedding, a large wash tub for bathing, candles, pillows, books and writing materials, a waterbed and a rubber boat. By the time all these supplies arrived, we were more than ready for everything.

Once the second load of supplies was delivered to the cabin, I was able to install the windows. I brought two window frames with the small 8 x10 glass sections in each one. Each window held nine panes of glass. I also brought two extra in case one or more broke. I had glass putty and a putty knife so I was able to install all the glass without breaking any. I then cut out the holes for the windows and installed them. I made each window so they could be opened and a breeze would ventilate the cabin. Once the windows were installed, the whole environment of the cabin changed. We had light during the day and it started to feel like a home.

I built a set of bunk beds for the kids as soon as I could. I put them in the far corner near the stove. I made extensions that slid into the ends of the beds. When we had visitors overnight, the beds would be long enough for an adult to sleep on. I also made a larger bed for Mary and me to sleep on. I put storage bins under the bed to put our clothing in. Once the foam padding arrived, the beds were quite warm and comfortable. I also built a counter with a small sink in it. I had stainless steel sheet metal and I rolled it over the counter to make an easy-to-clean work surface to prepare food on and to do dishes. I took the wooden crates that the chainsaw gas came in and attached them to the walls.

There were four crates and they made great cabinets to keep our pots, pans, plates and glasses in. I also built a shelf above the front door. The shelf was high up on the wall and one needed to stand on a ladder to get to it, but we stored a lot of our food up there, including two cans of honey. When you came into the cabin, located on the right was a small shelf I installed to put the shortwave radio on. We also mounted the first aid kit there and kept our music in that area.

I needed a shed to get all my outside gear protected and out of the rain as well as store some of the items from inside the cabin that we didn't need. I had plenty of black Griffolyn plastic. This plastic has nylon thread going through it to make it stronger. It also held up to the sun much better than regular Visqueen. I cut down several very small black spruce trees with a diameter of about 3-4 inches. I put together a frame and roof supports and then stapled the Visqueen to it; yes, I even brought a stapler. I built some benches inside of the shed to set my toolbox on. It became a great place to store the chainsaws, oil and gas. I also made the mistake of putting a bag of onions at the back of the shed. The size of the shed was about 8 feet x12 feet.

Food storage was worked out with a trap door into the underside of the cabin. I put a 3-foot x 3-foot trap door in the middle of the floor and then dug down about 2 feet into the ground. I wrapped the hole in Visqueen and voila! we had a deep hole refrigerator which stayed cold all summer long.

12

HERE COME THE BEARS

I was still working on the cabin when the first bear arrived. I just finished installing a dead bolt on the door and the two windows were installed on the front and West side of the cabin. There were no windows on the North and East side of the cabin. Of course, the noise was coming from the East side. It sounded like a ripping noise. That was the side the shed was on. I was in my underwear when I grabbed my Ruger pistol and went running out the door. It was about six o'clock in the morning when all this happened and the kids and Mary were still in bed. Mary was awake and knew I had gone outside. I ran out into the front yard of the cabin and looked back at my black Griffolyn shed. There was a long tear down the side of the shed facing me. There was no doubt what had caused the rip. The claw marks started with a large paw print on the plastic. The bear must have enjoyed the sound of the ripping plastic. I yelled at the bear to come out and he did.

In my helicopter days, we darted and tagged many bears in the Brooks Range. All the bears were grizzly bears. This bear was a black bear of much larger size than I had ever seen in this neck of the woods. I had my gun pointed down where I figured his head would come out of the shed. I was really surprised when his head came out at least a foot higher than where I was pointing the gun. My first thought was how far away from the door to the cabin I was. I knew bears were very fast. I had clocked one with the helicopter at 35 miles per hour. My distance to the door was about the same distance to the bear. He just looked right at me like: "what do you want?" He then turned around and went back into the shed. I yelled at him again and this time he came all the way out. He had just come out of hibernation and his black hair was long with a bright white diamond on his chest. His ears were up and the look on his face was still questioning what I wanted. The gun had six shots in it so I fired one over his head in hopes he would hear the noise and run off, but instead all he did was shake his head from the noise and start going back into the shed. In the cabin, I woke everyone up with that first shot. I don't know what he was wanting out of the shed except the onions, but I yelled at him again and fired a second round over his head. That seemed to get his attention and he turned back around and faced me again. I fired a third round over his head which must have been hurting his ears so he turned around and walked back into the woods. I have heard that if you shoot at a bear you should always save the last round for yourself, just in case the other rounds don't bring him down. I was still shaking when I went back into the cabin. Mary and the kids were all up. I guess the loud reports from the pistol made them a bit curious about what was going on outside. Since they saw none of what I saw, I had to explain to them several times what had happened. As soon as they were dressed, they all went outside to see the large rip in the Griffolyn. After that, everyone was on bear alert. This particular bear became a constant visitor to our cabin. He never got any food other than an onion or two and some lettuce, but he was always hanging around the area.

As the summer progressed, that same bear got into more of our stuff. We had the waterbed outside on the ground and had it filled full of water in case the channel in front of the cabin dried up, which it did later on in the summer. The big black bear got a big kick out of walking on the rubber bed but forgot to pull in his claws. I got up one morning and found the bed full of holes and flat on the ground with no water. I tried to fix it but it was beyond repair. Once I had parked my airplane out on the gravel bar, the same bear, later on in the summer, got curious about what I had in my supply box near the plane which was full of grease, oil, and butyrate dope used for repairing the plane's fabric. The bear bit into the butyrate dope can, puncturing the can, and I am sure he got a mouth full of the chemical. I found the punctured can on the ground a few feet away from the plane. Fortunately, the can was upright so most of the liquid was still in it. I covered the hole with gray tape; later in the summer I needed that butyrate dope to fix the airplane. At least he never bothered the plane after that incident.

Finally, one day I was working on building a kitchen table for the cabin. I had been working on it for a while. It was a sunny, warm day about noon. I happened to look down the trail that led to our small greenhouse located about 150 feet from the cabin. There came the big black bear right down the trail towards me. The kids were on the other side of the cabin so I yelled at them to get into the cabin and had Mary hand me all the guns we had. I used the pistol first and fired a round over his head. He didn't even slow down. I grabbed the shot gun and fired one barrel, a blast over his head again. By now he was less then 30 feet away. This time he stopped and turned sideways to me. I let him have it right in the rear with the other barrel of the 12-gauge shotgun. It must have hurt like hell. He let out a roar, turned around and ran back down the path. He jumped on our greenhouse, stomped on it, flattening it into the ground. After he did that, he stood up on his hind legs and walked like a human back into the woods. That was all it took. He stayed away from the cabin from then on. We would see him on the other side of the river rummaging around for berries to eat. He would look over at us but never came back to our side of the river. Just like a kid, once you set the rules they seem to understand.

Once we had the first encounter with the big black bear, I took the last two small replacement windows that were left over from the window job and put them into the North and East walls of the cabin. At least now if we ran out of the cabin we could check first to see what was out there. I installed the one in the back at bed-height which made it easy to just roll over and look out into the woods while lying in bed. One morning Mary and I were in bed when we were awakened by a scratching noise at the back of the cabin. I raised up and looked over the top of Mary and I could see fur going back and forth just under the small window. I told Mary to look out the window. She turned over and to her surprise there was a bear going back and forth against the cabin wall about six inches from her face. I expected her to at least say something of surprise, but by then she was pretty used to seeing the bears. All she said was: "that's pretty neat," turned over and went back to sleep.

On another morning, we were all awakened by the sound of our buckets hitting the side of the cabin. We all jumped out of bed and looked out the small window on the East side of the cabin and to our surprise there were two bears outside playing with one of our white buckets. They were tossing it around like a ball. One bear would catch the bucket and throw it up into the air and the other bear would try to catch the bucket. They rolled around on the ground with the bucket batting it all over the place. They played around outside for almost 30 minutes before they tired of it and went back into the woods. Fred and Michael were so intrigued with watching the bears. We all got some good laughs out of those bears and they didn't even hurt the bucket.

Later in the summer, when I was alone at the cabin, I got the idea to cross the river and climb the mountain on the other side. I could see from our side of the river a large plateau about half way up the mountain. I was curious what was on that plateau and what the view would be like. I had the small rubber raft with me, so I took it across the river and pulled it up into the brush. I then took off hiking and headed toward the top of the mountain.

I brought with me some canned fruit, a canteen of water and a sandwich in case I got hungry. I found a fairly nice trail going up the spine of the mountain, so I followed it. About noon, I was getting hungry so stopped at a large rock and began to eat my sandwich. I brought binoculars with me, so I scanned the area. I just happened to look down the way I had just come up. About 100 yards off I noticed movement. When I zoomed in on the movement I spotted a large grizzly bear on the same trail I had just walked. He had his nose in the air and was definitely following my scent. I think I said "Oh shit" or something like that. I quickly jumped off the rock and headed straight down the mountain. I was above the plateau so I headed down toward the plateau. I must have made it down in record time. It was a very nice plateau with a great view. It looked to be about ten acres in size. Of course, my interest in the plateau was being nixed by the bear which I was positive was following me. I just kept going across the plateau and down the other side.

I ended up on a very steep rock scree that led almost all the way to the river. I was almost able to sit down and slide on by butt. The rocks were very loose so I just slid down the mountain as the rocks gave out from under me. It was a quick trip down to the river. I then walked back to my rubber raft, always looking over my shoulder. I know how fast a bear can run. I got back to the raft without any problem and floated back across the river. I was very happy to make it back to the cabin.

One day we were all in the cabin eating some lunch when we heard something heavy up on our roof. It was digging into our roof so I assumed it was a bear. I yelled for the bear to get off our roof. I grabbed the pistol and out the door I ran. Well to my surprise the bear came off the roof at the same time and place as I exited the door and almost landed on me. We were face to face and my first reaction was to pull the trigger on the gun. I must have grazed the bear's foot. All I remember was this terrified look on the bear's face as it tried to leave the area like a rocket. The dirt flew up against me and the door as the bear's feet dug in. I realized the bear was only a small female and I had just scared it to death. I can't say I was not as scared as the bear, but it all happened so fast. Once the bear was gone, I noticed some blood on the ground. Fortunately, not a lot of blood but I followed the trail back into the woods until the blood disappeared. I felt terrible that I had wounded the bear, but I was sure in the end I only grazed her leg or foot. After we were sure the bear had kept running, Mary got a good laugh out of the look on my face at the time of the incident.

Throughout the summer we would see bears in the area. Sometimes near the cabin and sometimes out in the flats near the river. Once in a while, we would see them when we were hiking. I believe to this day not killing a bear was our salvation. Others in the valley said they were forced to kill bears because they were on their porch or pushing against their door. Later their cabins were broken into by bears. My cabin was still untouched 10 years later when I returned. Bears are very smart animals and not to be trusted, but yet, in my experience, I have found them to be more curious than anything else. They will avoid contact with humans unless they are fed. They love garbage dumps and when visiting Bornite, I have counted as many as six bears at the Bornite dump.

Bears are also opportunistic animals and will take advantage of any situation where they can get free food. One time at the Bornite kitchen, a bear figured out how to get over the split back door of the kitchen. He then figured out how to open the huge commercial refrigerator by pulling on the large handle. That bear was in and out of the building with a steak in his jaws like nobody's business. He did that twice in two days while everyone was eating their breakfast. Finally, one of the guys who was staying there installed a hot wire across the split door. The bear, on his next attempt, laid his paws on the wire and the electric shock knocked him back. He let out a growl and took off running never to try that again.

13

VISITORS FROM ALL OVER

One would think so far out in the wilderness that visitors would be a very rare occasion. Well, I must admit I was surprised at just how many people came to our small cabin. I think by the time we left the cabin we had 47 different people visit us. The first visitors who arrived were Bill Murkley and a partial crew of folks headed for work at the next valley over. They were on their way to the camp from Fairbanks. Gordon had asked them to make a stop and check on us. It was near the middle of May when I heard a helicopter coming towards the cabin. I went out, sat with my camera and took a photograph as they flew low over the top of the building. We hadn't heard that much noise in over a month. They circled around and landed on the gravel bar across from the cabin. They brought beer, soda pop and Kentucky Fried Chicken with them. When Fred and Michael saw the chicken, I thought they would eat it all themselves. I can still see Michael walking around in his blue and white jacket, red stocking cap with knitted tie ropes hanging down over his ears and a chicken leg in each hand. This was the happiest I had seen him since we arrived. The guys had put the beer in the creek in front of the cabin and it didn't take long to get cold as the river still had ice in the water.

We drug out every chair and log that we had to sit on. We were starving for news from the outside world. Jimmy Carter was making some kind of peace agreement between the Palestinians and Israel. Seemed like I'd heard that before. Turned out to be a fun party and everyone, including the kids, had a great time and we stayed up pretty late that night. The days were getting very long by then. The guys were staying just over in the next valley about 25 minutes away from us. They flew back to their camp that night and left us to the quiet of the wilderness once again.

As soon as the river shed its ice, but was still high enough for a boat to travel up past our cabin, three people arrived. They were headed up river to other cabins located along the Ambler River. Most of the cabins up river from us were owned by environmentalists. One cabin was owned by someone who was a "Friends of the Earth", another was "The Sierra Club", another from "The Wilderness Society" and others who were strict environmentalists. They had all built their cabins before we built ours.

I went down to welcome them at the river when they arrived but soon found myself defending my lifestyle. They started out asking questions about how I had acquired the land. Seems like they had acquired their land all at the same time. I told them I was there when their land was staked, remembering the jars that were nailed to the trees up and down the valley all dated the same date. That surprised them as I am sure they were not aware of anyone knowing about the float trip made a few years ago. They complained that I was supporting the oil companies with my helicopters and the helicopter was doing more damage to the environment than just about anything else. I said "yes, we do work with the oil companies at times, but we also support geologists, BLM, Forest Service, police, and miners". I could tell they weren't listening to me and even told me they had threatened to burn down my cabin before I returned this last year. I finally told them that they should leave because we were not getting anywhere with the conversation. I walked with them down to their boat. I then pointed out the oil slick which was coming out of their motor and flowing down the river. I told them that at least my helicopter left no sign it had ever been there.

The problem I find with overzealous environmentalists is they are human, just as I am. When a human is put in a pristine area, soon it will look like trash. They flew their garbage out thinking they were doing the best thing for the valley. I buried or burned my garbage. They shot bears when their cabins were threatened. I never shot and killed anything except a squirrel. They also admitted to their dogs killing some rare birds and destroyed their nests. I taught my boys to respect the wilderness and be aware of things that could kill you. The bottom line is people try to tell other people to do things that they themselves cannot possibly do. They hide behind the title environmentalist, but in real life they are still people, doing the same things that honest people try not to do.

They ended up visiting our cabin later on in the summer and this time, they were much friendlier than the first visit. We even visited them later and had a good time. I guess people make assumptions about other people without even knowing who they are or what story they bring to the table. Once they find out the truth, they begin to communicate and soon they find a new friend. One other comment on this subject is when you are alone in the wilderness and something bad happens to you, those same people may be the only ones to save you. It's nice to have a helicopter nearby, because it may just save your life!

One day the kids were playing out on the gravel bar in front of the cabin. We could watch them from the front window of the cabin. Suddenly they both came running up the bank to tell us that a man was walking up the river toward the cabin. I went outside and sure enough here came a big man all bent over with a huge pack on his back. I waited until he was almost to the cabin and yelled hello over to him. I startled him and it was then that I realized he had not seen the kids or the cabin. He came up the bank and greeted both Mary and me. He was very surprised to find a family all alone so far from anything. He hardly spoke any English, he was from Sweden. It took us a while to understand him. He had quite a story to tell us. We could not even begin to pronounce his name so we just called him The Swede.

His story began when he arrived in Anchorage in early March 1978. He decided he wanted to walk across Alaska to the Arctic Ocean. He outfitted himself in Anchorage and even had supplies flown out to small villages where he would be going through on his journey. Everything went good for the first couple months of his journey. It took him four months of walking to make it to Nome, Alaska. He said while in Nome, he was to rest up for a few days and resupply from a shipment which was supposed to be waiting there for him. When he arrived, he was unable to find his supplies. Something or someone had taken the supplies. He had very little money left so he bought what he could and headed back out on the trail. When he got to us he was about out of food and was getting very hungry. We cooked up a great meal for him and gave him a place to sleep on the floor. He turned out to be a very nice man and stayed with us for about a week. He wanted to continue on but his feet were about wore out and he had lost too much weight. We showed him on a map where he was and how much farther he would need to go. It just so happened that Bill Murkley flew over to tell us about a Fourth of July party that was happening in a couple of days. He was willing to pick us all up with the helicopter and take us to Bornite where the party was being held. The Swede made a decision right then and there that his trip was over. He wanted to go back home. The day of the party he went with all of us to Bornite. He stayed for the party and then caught a ride over to Kobuk where he took another flight back to Anchorage and then home.

Other visitors were camp folks who were there for the season and just came over to visit us. Mary was a very striking lady and I am sure they just wanted some time with a lady. They also found out I was a helicopter mechanic and would stop by with their helicopters to ask questions or get some small maintenance item taken care of. Ray Houseman was also working in the area and every chance he could, he would stop by for a cup of coffee or a sweet roll. My only complaint with him was he never shut down the helicopter. It would just set out there running while we sat in the cabin and told stories about what was going on in the area.

I strung a thin wire up and into the trees spanning several yards. This was the antenna for the shortwave radio. Once we had the shortwave radio up and running we could talk to Bornite. That meant talking to Jim Gillespie. He was the Bornite mine camp boss and also the camp organizer. He was a super nice man and was always willing to help us with anything we needed. We could call him on the radio and ask him how things were going and he would go off on some story that just made you laugh. He got the biggest kick out of our adventures at the cabin.

Jim was also a great pilot and owned a Cessna 170-B. One beautiful, clear evening he flew out to our cabin and landed on our gravel bar just to say hello. Well actually, he had heard it was Fred's 5th birthday, so he brought out a chocolate cake his wife made from scratch at his Bornite home. He also brought a half gallon of chocolate ice cream. When he showed up at the cabin with all those goodies, a birthday party started. I will never forget the smile on Fred's face when he saw the cake and ice cream.

Jim stayed until it was getting late. We walked him out to his airplane on the gravel bar and said our goodbyes. He got into the airplane, turned the key to start it and nothing happened. The battery was dead. I had to hand start the airplane for him. The airplane was a tail dragger, so the nose was very high in the air. I could barely reach the propeller. We turned off the magnetos and turned the prop straight across. I grabbed ahold of the prop and gave it all I had. The first pull failed to start. The next pull it started with a loud roar and I was sure I was going to be eaten by that propeller. I actually fell backwards to get away from it. Up in the cockpit, Jim missed the whole event. Once he saw I was clear of the airplane he took off down the gravel bar and lifted off into the air. He then gave us a mini airshow as he proceeded to do loops and rolls right over the river. Then with a dip of his wing he left and flew back to Bornite 15 miles away. Jim really made Mary and me feel much safer with the kids just knowing he was there.

One time we had left the cabin for a day trip of hiking and when we got back there was a note on the cabin door. We also found wooden stakes in the ground with red flagging all around them. It seemed that while we were away, Sunshine Mining stopped by and staked the mineral rights to the ground under the cabin. I knew there was a copper vein that led out into the river, but it had never entered my mind that I didn't get the mineral rights to the land when I staked it. The note explained everything, they were going through this area and decided to land and say hello. When they found we weren't there, they staked the land anyway. To this day I am not sure if it was for real or just fooling around.

At the end of summer when the camps were closing down for the winter, a helicopter arrived full of food for Mary and me. They gave us steaks, frozen shrimp and lots of canned goods. We were only going to be there ourselves for just a few more days but they wouldn't take no for answer. I can only say that we really ate good that last week we were at the cabin. I guess it goes to show you that even in the wilderness, stuff just comes out of the sky.

14

BRINGING OUT THE AIRPLANE.

Once the cabin was made into a home, Mary and I decided we could use the airplane at the cabin. Getting mail and fresh supplies from the town of Kobuk along the Kobuk River was impossible without the airplane. The town of Kobuk was about 40 miles away. I found out from Bill Murkley that fuel would be delivered to the Bornite strip for the contract he was working on. The pilot who flew the fuel in was working with Sunshine Helicopters that year. I arranged to be picked up at the cabin by Bill on the day the fuel arrived so I could fly back to Circle City with the fuel plane. When the day came for me to leave, it was with mixed emotions, mostly of trepidation, but I needed to get supplies. I remember Mary standing outside the cabin with the two kids waving at me as I climbed in the helicopter to go over to Bornite. Mary, who had never been around small kids much, especially kids as young as Fred and Michael, was going to be all alone with them for several days waiting for my return. What if something happened to me, what would she do? Once again not a complaint from her, just a very worried look on her face.

The flight back to Circle City was without incident. We arrived late in the afternoon on a very cloudy day. After checking in with Gordon and filling him in on how thing were going out at the cabin and him filling me in on how things were going at the company, I went back down to my small cabin there in Circle City. The next morning, I went down to the Circle City runway and looked over my airplane making sure it was in good condition to fly. After I had soloed the year before, my flying time had been very limited. The demand for working on the helicopters and the coming winter restricted my flying to almost nothing. I was a very inexperienced pilot. Still I was confident that I could fly the airplane to my cabin at the Ambler River.

I knew I had only 600 feet of gravel bar to land on at the cabin. I paced off 600 feet of runway at Circle City, put a stake in the ground at the 600-foot mark then fired up the airplane and took off. The first three attempts at landing were total failures. I just kept going past the mark, sometimes by quite a long distance. Finally, on the fourth attempt I got the airplane down and stopped just a few feet past the stake. That gave me hope I could actually land successfully. I made another attempt and this time I got the airplane stopped right at the 600-foot mark. I said to myself: "good to go."

I went over to the Yukon Trading Post with my list of groceries and bought two bottles of wine, some cheese, meat, and fresh vegetables. I then went down to my cabin in Circle City, picked up some other things we needed at the Ambler cabin and put them into the airplane. I then topped off the fuel tanks, said my goodbyes and took off back to the Ambler River cabin. I was only in Circle City for three days, but I felt like I had been gone a lot longer.

I left Circle around noon and flew towards Bettles, Alaska, which was the half way point to the cabin. The weather at takeoff was good, but as I flew West, the wind began to pick up. The Taylorcraft is a very light airplane and is affected by wind like a kite. The flight became pretty rough and I was being bounced around like a ping pong ball. By the time I got to Bettles, the wind was blowing about 30 miles per hour. I pointed my nose into the wind and lined up with the 5,000-foot runway, cut the power and headed for the end of the runway. Soon I was adding power because I was going backwards. I had to fly the plane against the wind to land. When I touched down I had to hold power just to taxi to the end where the fuel pumps were located. I found that shutting off the aircraft was not a good idea because the wind wanted to pick it up and take off with it. I don't know what I would have done if there had not been someone at the fuel pump. The man saw I was having difficulties so he came out and held the plane while I shut it down. It took both of us to get it over to the fuel pumps. We tied it down while he added fuel.

Once I was all topped off with fuel I asked him where I could park, as taking off in the wind would have been a waste of my time. He helped me get it over to a tie down area and we secured the plane. I thanked him and then went over to the lodge where I had dinner. I ended up sleeping in the tail of the airplane that night and woke up around 4 am to winds that had died down to almost nothing. The sun was already up so I decided it was time to move on. I untied the airplane and taxied out to the runway and took off.

The wind was calm and the flight was smooth; not a cloud in the sky. I was flying about 1,500 feet when I switched tanks to transfer fuel from my wing tank to the nose tank. The nose tank has a rod that floats on a cork. When the rod gets down to the top of the fuel cap you are out of fuel. The rod was about 2 inches from the cap when I started to transfer fuel. Normally the rod would start to go up as the fuel entered from the wing tank, but this did not happen. The rod continued to go down. I was at a loss as to why I was running out of fuel when I had just filled the tank the night before. I tried shaking the wings, but to no avail. I put the plane into a dive, still no results. Now I began to worry. There is no place to land out there over the river so I flew on hoping against hope that I could somehow make it to Bornite. The gas gauge continued to drop until it was laying on the top of the gas cap. Still the engine motored on. I began to sweat as I scanned the distance for a glimpse of Bornite. Suddenly I saw the Bornite strip off in the distance. I made a direct approach as I was sure the engine would quit before I could get there. Finally, I reached the point when I knew the engine could quit and I would still make the runway. I made a beautiful landing and as I touched down, the engine coughed and died. At the same time, I realized that fuel was starting to transfer into the nose tank and the rod started going up. I got out of the plane and I looked up at the wing tank fuel cap. The fuel cap has a short tube that runs out of the top of the cap and bends towards the direction of flight. To my surprise, stuck in the end of the vent was a bumble bee. The bumble bee had literally plugged the fuel vent causing a vacuum and shutting the fuel off from coming out of the wing tank. I guess when I landed and stopped the plane it allowed the bee to become loose enough to start the fuel to flow. I climbed up where I could reach the cap and cleared the dead bee out of the vent. I came so close to not making my destination. I envisioned the newspaper head-line: Death By Bumble Bee!

I took off from Bornite as soon as I had a full nose tank. The plane started on the first pull of the propeller. It was still pretty early in the morning since I had left Bettles at four o'clock in the morning. I flew the 15 miles out to the cabin in no time at all. I buzzed the cabin and then went around to make my approach onto my short little gravel bar. In my first attempt, the plane bounced too high and floated too far. I gave it the gas and went around for another try. Once again the plane floated too far and I was forced to go around again. By now Mary and the kids were outside watching the show. I am sure they thought I would soon crash in the river. On the third try I was able to touch down right at the end of the gravel bar. I bounced once, floated a distance, then touched down again with my brakes on as hard as I could push. If it had been a paved runway, the plane would have flipped over. The loose gravel on the gravel bar let the airplane wheels slide along until I slowed down enough to do a ground loop at the very end of the bar. The tail wheel actually went into the river. I taxied out of the river and over to a parking spot I had set up for the plane on a higher piece of ground. I got out and into the arms of Mary and both the kids. They were so happy to see me in one piece. I tied down the airplane and pulled out the stuff that I had brought. We then went up to the cabin and had breakfast, complete with fresh milk. Later that day we had a great dinner of steak and fresh vegetables, salad and wine for the adults. I must admit, it was several weeks before I had the courage to fly off the gravel bar again.

15

THE JOY OF FLYING

I landed back on that gravel bar many times but the thirteenth time was the worst landing. But before I get to that landing, I must tell you about some of our other adventures. About every two weeks, I would take the airplane and fly over to Kobuk. They had a small dirt strip on the back side of town and it seemed like every time a plane landed, several people would gather at the strip to see who was coming in. On one of the landings, there was a pretty good cross wind and when I touched down I bounced and the plane floated onto the edge of the airstrip. Before I could get it back under control, I managed to take out several small willows with the prop and put some green stains on the left wing. The people standing alongside of the runway got a real kick out of my imperfect landing. Many times, when I would come back to the village and they realized it was me they would gather to see if I would give them another show. Fortunately, it never happened again after that.

It was a fairly short walk from the strip to the village store and Post Office. It was always exciting to get mail and occasionally a package. We did buy some things at the store, but being a village store the cost of things was quite high. Still if you needed something and the store happened to have it, it was nice to know you could buy it.

The town also had a local satellite phone station. The state had put the phones in all the villages in the early 70's. Only one phone for each village, located in a small heated building, sometimes at the store and sometimes in a building by itself. Whatever the building, it needed a large satellite dish on its roof or nearby on a tower. When one went to use the phone, there may or may not be a line. The cost of the call was free which to me was amazing. It was a fantastic convenience for the people of the villages. For Mary and me, this was a great way to check in with our families and keep them informed as to how we were coping with living in the wilderness. Whenever I flew over to Kobuk I would go alone and Mary would stay behind to care for the kids. I never did fly with the kids in the airplane. I guess I just didn't have the confidence to put them in harm's way with my flying abilities. As for Mary, once the kids left to go back to Fairbanks she was free to fly with me anywhere we wanted to go.

The boys stayed with us until the July 4th party at Bornite. When we took the Swede over to Bornite for him to leave, the boys were with us. After the party, Bill Murkley was flying the helicopter back to Circle City for some maintenance. He offered to take the kids back with him and make sure they got back to Fairbanks to stay with their grandmother. For Mary and me it was a chance to get out and do more with the airplane, as well as longer hikes out into the wilderness. We took hikes with the boys but only as far as we could go and still get back to the cabin before nightfall.

The airplane gave us the ability to take trips up the Ambler River on nights that were calm and beautiful. One evening we took a trip up the valley toward the Noatak River up near the North Slope. It was one of those amazing nights with no wind. The sun was low on the horizon at nine in the evening. The flight was smooth and almost mystic. We saw mountains and valleys that few people ever see. By the time we got back and landed at the gravel bar, Mary and I had a whole new appreciation of where we were.

A few days after the kids were gone, we took the airplane over to Dahl Creek airstrip. It is a very long and wide airstrip that at one time was used by Wien Airlines to deliver goods and services to this remote area of Alaska. The building at the end of the airstrip was a store bought, manufactured log looking log cabin. They used it as their airstrip terminal for many years. We landed and taxied down to the opposite end of the runway where some old cabins from a long deserted mine existed. We found an old road that followed a creek up into the hills to the North of the airstrip. Mary grabbed our small packs and our gold pans and away we went, hiking up the road for several miles. We found an area along the creek that looked promising for gold panning. We spent several hours trying our luck at panning but with little result. We finally gave up and walked up the road further until we reached an old jade mine. I heard about this mine and how the guy who worked the jade mine lived in Arizona. There was a huge rock saw and several old jade boulders laying here and there and old equipment was everywhere. We even saw the wooden sled used to bring the boulders out of the creek. Activity at the jade mine would typically begin early spring before the melt off where a wooden sled was pulled across the snow-covered frozen land by a small crawler. Boulders were pulled from areas identified on a map from the summer before. The large jade boulders would be pried out of the creeks or off the mountains, loaded on the sled and brought back to the mine. The guy from Arizona would spend the summer cutting the boulders into smaller pieces preparing them for shipment back to Arizona. After he had enough jade, he would head back to Arizona where he and his wife would make beautiful jade jewelry.

Mary and I were not equipped to carry any large pieces of jade, but we did find some small broken chunks around on the ground. We put a few pebbles into our back packs and headed back to the airplane. It took us about an hour and a half to walk back, but the weather was good and the hike was worth the trip. Once back at the airplane we loaded up the packs, Mary stood on the brakes and I hand propped the airplane. Once we got the plane started, we taxied out on the very long runway and took off into the sky heading back to the cabin. It was a great, adventurous day but still good to get back to the cabin and cook up a meal.

Around the end of July, Mary received word of a huge family reunion back in Rochester, Minnesota. She told me she was very anxious to go. It was the first time in years that the family would all be back together. We had been without the kids for a couple weeks, and had been on several adventures together. I really hated to see her leave, but I could understand her situation so I agreed to fly her back to Fairbanks so she could catch a flight out to Minnesota. We took off around July 25th on a very nice morning. I had a 55-gallon gas barrel that was flown in shortly after I got the airplane to the cabin. I topped off the fuel tanks and we departed for Fairbanks. The flight was smooth and we had a bit of a tailwind so we made it from the cabin all the way to Fairbanks on the one load of fuel. We landed at Metro Field Airport in Fairbanks. There were plenty of spots to tie down and I knew several of the people who worked around the airfield. I caught a ride for Mary to the airport and sent her on her way. I wasn't too sure she would be coming back, she wasn't too sure either. I spent some time visiting my two boys and bought some more supplies for the cabin. I ended up spending about 5 days in Fairbanks before heading back to the cabin.

16

HOW NOT TO LAND
ON A GRAVEL BAR

It was August 1ˢᵗ when I left Fairbanks for the flight back to the
cabin. I would need to top off with fuel at Bettles. The weather
was good all the way to Bettles. After I refueled the plane and got
back into the air, I noticed some rather large thunderheads building up right in the center of my flight path. I was sure I would
be knocked out of the air if I flew anywhere near those storms. I
turned North in the direction that would take me over the Brooks
Range. This would keep me well clear of the storms. The problem of course was the underpowered airplane I was flying. It
takes quite a while to climb up to 6,000 feet which I needed to do
just to get over the mountain range. I finally made it over to the
other side and found myself in very unfamiliar territory.

I turned West and followed a long wide pass toward the direction of the cabin. I was in a descent back to 1,500 feet when
the engine coughed and quit. My first thought was "where am I
going to land when all that is below me are hills and trees…lots

of trees". I had also not included this route in my flight briefing. If I went down out here I would never be found. At least I didn't panic as my flight training kicked in and I remembered the carburetor ice lever. Pushing this lever in would supply the warm air to the carburetor. I immediately did this and in only a few seconds the engine caught and started running again. I must admit, my adrenaline was pumping and I felt very alone. Once the engine was back to purring along I started trying to find my bearings. Nothing looked familiar and my sectional was not helping me find my location. I figured I needed to keep going West and I would eventually find the Kobuk River or the ocean. As the plane droned on at a speedy 90 knots, I kept looking to both sides for something familiar. I was starting to panic a little because my fuel was getting low and the sun was going down. Then I spotted sand dunes. What a beautiful, but very strange site out in the middle of nowhere Alaska. I knew right away I was seeing the Kobuk Sand Dunes which is a large expanse of sand spread out over many miles of the West end of the Brooks Range. I turned the airplane South and after just a little while, I recognized the Ambler River and soon the Bornite airstrip – I heaved a sigh of relief.

I went ahead and followed the Ambler on up to the cabin. I was surprised to see that the river was very high. I guess in the 5 days I had been gone it had been raining a lot. Tonight, though, it was sunny and the winds were very calm, a typical late summer evening in Alaska. The river was covering both ends of my gravel strip and the water was flowing in front of the cabin at a fairly strong clip. I probably should have just turned around and went back to Bornite, but I was tired and looking forward to my own bed and I felt that my abilities were up to the task of landing on my shortened airstrip. I circled once feeling out the wind situation. I decided I would float in over the water and just as my wheels were over the gravel end of the bar, I would touch down and slam on my brakes. I went out quite a distance and down the river so I could make a long, slow, straight-in approach. I could not feel any wind in the valley so it really should have worked. I turned the aircraft around and was at about 300 feet. I aimed the nose at the end of the gravel bar and made my approach. It all looked very good until about 50 feet from the end of the gravel bar when the plane just dropped out of the sky and into the river. The motor was at idle so the propeller was turning at very low RPM. As soon as the wheels hit the water, the airplane flipped over onto its top. It happened so fast I didn't even have time to panic. The strong current immediately started taking the plane and me down river. Luckily this section of river was an inside bend and the plane was headed toward the bank. I climbed out of the upside down plane and ran down the underside of the right wing. I still had not even gotten wet. I was able to jump from the end of the wing to the river bank. The river bank was about four feet above the water level, just the right height to grab hold of the tail as it went by. I first reached over and grabbed the right wing which pulled me into the river. Now I was wet! The engine was heavy and began filling full of water so it was sinking and the tail was coming up. That's when I was able to get a grip on the tail. Since the tail and the bank were at the perfect height, I was able to put both arms under the tail and actually lift the plane up against the bank. I just kept working it closer to the bank until I was sure the river wouldn't take it away. I then went over to where the plane was supposed to be tied down and grabbed some rope, came back over to the plane and tied it off to some small trees and bushes on the old gravel bar. I climbed down and emptied out the airplane. To my surprise, the cockpit never got wet and everything I brought with me was not damaged. I gathered up all the stuff and headed over to the cabin. I had to wade across the now flowing slough in front of the cabin. Boy was I ready to get into some dry clothes and eat a good meal. Out of exhaustion, I slept like a baby that night.

17

HOW TO BUSH-FIX AN AIRPLANE

The next day I went over and checked on the airplane and saw the river had gone down quite a bit overnight. Still, the engine was under water but the plane remained secure to the bank. I went back over to the cabin and heated up the stove so I could make a fresh loaf of bread. Making bread also allowed me to think about how I was going to get my airplane out of the river. Luckily for me, I had friends in the area.

Sometime in the afternoon, I heard a helicopter in the area. I went outside and here came Ray Houseman over the hill. He must have seen the airplane upside down against the bank and quickly went into a dive and landed out on the gravel bar. He got out and looked over toward the cabin where he saw me waving at him. He came straight over and made sure I was alright. I offered him some hot chocolate and fresh bread and then told him what happened. We went together out to the airplane and he looked over the situation. He told me about a new helicopter working in the area that could most likely pick the whole plane up and out of the water and put it back down on the gravel bar. He said he would contact the man that day and see if his schedule would allow him to break loose for a while so he could come over and get the plane out of the river.

The next morning a new McDonnell Douglas 500-D model arrived. The pilot's name was Todd and he was a very nice man. He told me he had talked with Ray and figured it shouldn't take very long to get the aircraft out of the water. We quickly took everything out of the helicopter that we could in order to lighten the load. I then attached long straps to the Taylorcraft's trailing edge wing roots. He hovered over the aircraft and I hooked the straps up to the cargo hook on the belly of the helicopter. At first the helicopter strained to move the plane, but as he lifted the load the water began to pour out of the engine compartment. As the water drained, the plane got lighter, and Todd was able to lift it up and out of the river. He then hovered over to the gravel bar where I had indicated I wanted the airplane. The problem was the airplane was still upside down. I had Todd hover while I attached a rope to the tail wheel. Once that was done, I pulled the plane over so the wheels were facing down. Todd lowered the plane to the ground and released the cargo hook. Then he set down so we could put all the stuff back into his helicopter. The whole event lasted about 45 minutes. He said he needed to get back as he told everyone back at camp he would only be gone for an hour. I offered to pay him and he said one day he might need some maintenance done on the aircraft and since I happened to be school trained on that particular helicopter, he would bring it by if need be. As it turned out, he never returned.

I walked over to the airplane and assessed the damage after Todd had left. Besides the engine being filled with water, I noticed the metal propeller was bent. The nose cowling around the engine was caved in on the bottom and the fabric which covered the landing gear struts was torn away. The right wing was damaged out on the tip and the tail top bow was also damaged. The worst damage was the twisted and bent engine mount. I knew I had to get to work on the plane right away. If Mary came back we would need the airplane.

The first thing I did was drain the water out of the engine. Then I went to the river with one of my five gallon buckets and got clean river water. I poured the water through the engine until I was convinced I had clean water coming out of the engine. I went back to the cabin and got several quarts of chain bar oil and put that in the engine. I pulled the propeller through several times making sure it had circulated throughout the engine. I let that set overnight. The next day I went out and drained out the chain bar oil and replaced it with aircraft engine oil. I then made sure the carburetor and magnetos were dry. I turned the magneto switch to the on position and pulled the propeller through until the engine started. I ran the engine for about 15 minutes until it was warm, making sure I had oil pressure. I then shut it off, drained out the oil and added another fresh batch of oil to the engine. I started the engine again and let it run for another 15 minutes. Once I was satisfied the engine was going to be alright, I shut it off.

I went into the woods and cut off three long poles of black spruce. I took some rope and made a tripod that was centered over the airplane engine and unhooked all the cables and wires from the engine, removed the bolts holding it to the firewall, and with a come along winch, I removed the engine with the frame mount. The firewall was undamaged but the engine frame was bent and needed to be repaired so I removed the frame from the engine. That evening I called the Bornite mine and talked to Jim Gillespie. I told him what happened and asked if one of his welders at the mine could fix my engine mount. He said he would fly over later in the evening and pick it up. I made an exact pattern from the fire wall mounting holes on a piece of cardboard and gave that to him with the mount when he came over. I also asked him if he could call Gordon in Circle City and have him ship my wooden propeller and the bolts which were in my cabin at Circle. He agreed to do that, took my mount and left for Bornite.

I had cotton fabric and the butyrate dope to repair the damaged right wing. Since I had my aircraft toolbox with me, I had all the tools I needed to fix the airplane. I used river rocks to bend the metal on the nose cowling back into shape. I used my tools and some homemade wooden forms to fix the wing tip and the tail bow. Bornite had my engine mount finished and painted within a week's time. Once my wooden propeller arrived from Circle City, Jim Gillespie flew back over and delivered all I needed to put the airplane back together. The welder at Bornite did such a great job fixing the engine mount that it looked brand new and even the bolts went into the firewall without any binding. Once again, they wanted nothing for the work they had done. I tried to pay Jim but he would have none of it.

The crash occurred on August 1st, and by September 1st, I had the airplane back together. I ran the plane up and took it for a test flight over to Bornite and back. There was a little vibration from the wooden propeller but for the most part, it flew just fine. I entered all the work I had done on the airplane in the log books and then I stamped the work off with my A & P repair license number and signature. I even brought out some blue paint which matched the airplane colors so I painted the wing tip and the tail bow, touched up the landing gear struts and the engine cowling. When I was finished with the repairs, no one could tell the plane had been in an accident. After the accident, I was no longer afraid of the gravel bar. Once you have crashed your airplane, it's like you got that part of flying out of the way and now you can fly anyplace and land anywhere without fear.

A couple of days after getting the airplane finished, I got a call from Jim that Mary was in Fairbanks and she was ready for a ride back to the cabin. Mary was able to get a back to Bornite and I gave her a ride from there back out to the cabin. It was very, very good to see Mary again. I waited until after we made a great landing on the gravel bar before I told her about my accident on the return trip from dropping her off in Fairbanks. I guess she knew me well enough by then to just accept the whole story as another day at the cabin. Her only concern was for my safety and if I had been hurt.

18

GOLD PANNING AND CLOUDS

In September, toward the end of our visit at the cabin, Mary and I made plans for new adventures. One of the day time adventures was a float trip down the Ambler River. We had a two-man rubber raft I brought up on one of our trips into Fairbanks. One beautiful morning we decided to walk up the Ambler River about six miles toward the northern-most cabin in the valley. The cabin belonged to Molly and her husband. They built a very nice cabin a short distance off the river. This trip gave Mary and me a chance to visit most of the other homesteads in the valley.

As we walked along carrying our deflated rubber raft, trying to stay on the river gravel bar for easier walking, we kept an eye out for other cabins and bears. We knew of one cabin which was built on the bluff where I had been fishing when I first discovered the jar on the tree. We actually visited this cabin earlier in the summer and met the two people who had built it. They were no longer there, but still we stopped since it was a nice place to rest. As we continued up the valley, we spotted a mud hut built on the opposite side of the river. This, I later found out, belonged to Jim Kowalski. His cabin was very unique because he made a wood frame and then covered it with dirt and moss which made it blend into the surrounding area. Two more log cabins were built so far off the river that we passed right by them without even seeing them.

We finally reached Molly's cabin and met up with Molly and her husband. We stayed long enough with them to have lunch and share some wine. After many stories, the afternoon was wearing on so we put air in our raft and said our goodbyes. Once the raft was in the river, it was a quick six miles floating down to our cabin. The day was sunny and warm and the river only had a few rough spots along the way. It was a great float trip and we both had a ball.

After that trip, we had been contemplating a hiking trip up into the Brooks Range mountains. I wanted to try our hand at some more gold panning. I built a small portable riffle screen with carpet on it to catch gold if there was any. We had a small two-person tent, sleeping bags, guns and food. We spent a couple of days getting ready. Once our packs were loaded, we left the cabin and headed up river a distance and then turned East toward the taller mountains. Mary was quite a sight with her 80-pound pack on her back, a .41 mag gun strapped to her hip and a large brimmed hat on her head. As for me, my pack was only about 50 pounds with the portable riffle board strapped to my back and an old Aussie military wide brim hat on my head. We made quite a couple of Alaskan sourdoughs marching off into the woods.

We hiked off the river about one mile and came across one of the missing cabins. This cabin was owned by a Swedish couple who, at the time, were not there. They would work at jobs all summer and then spend the winters in the valley. Eventually they moved full time into the valley and raised a family at that cabin. Their cabin was a very nice, large cabin with a beautiful tall high cache. The cabin was located on a small lake which Mary and I had to walk around. Fortunately, there were some fairly good animal trails to follow and soon we were past the lake and into the foot hills leading up into a valley. We hiked all day and toward the end of the day we made it up into a large V-shaped valley. We pitched our little tent and got out our cook stove and made dinner. At that time of the year, the nights were beginning to be dark. We were already pretty tired, so after dinner we just hung out at the tent and eventually climbed into our sleeping bags and went to sleep.

We woke up to a beautiful morning. We fixed some breakfast and then went to work trying our luck at gold panning the little creek which ran down the valley near our tent. I brought a small folding shovel with me, so I began shoveling gravel and rocks from the creek into the riffle board. I set up the riffle board so part of the creek ran right over it. We spent several hours playing around in the very cold water. I was finally tired of shoveling and tired of being cold and wet, so we checked out our carpet for gold flakes. I would like to say right here and now that we hit the motherload, but alas, it was all for naught. No gold! As we sat there warming up in the sun and drying off, we realized the gold was the world around us.

It was an amazing valley and impossible to describe. We decided to leave the tent right where it was and wander off to explore the valley. We hiked up on a rocky outcrop high up on the hills which reminded me of alpine mountains. We spotted a pure white caribou all alone standing at the edge of the rock outcropping we were headed for. Then we spotted another caribou that looked almost black against the sky. We soon realized these two were a pair and they were hanging out together up there in the mountains. As we climbed up to the top of the hill, the caribou wandered away from us, but stayed within sight.

Once we reached the top of the mountain the view came into focus. We could see down into the Ambler River Valley. The whole South end of the valley spread out before us. We could see down to where the cabin was located but could not make out the cabin itself. It was such a clear and beautiful day, the mountains where the Bornite mine was located, 15+ miles away, could be seen. We continued to spend more time exploring the mountain top and that's when we spotted the arch. Slightly over the Western edge of the mountain, looking down into the valley, was this huge stone arch. Mary and I could not believe what we were seeing. The arch, not quite as large as the one in Arizona, was still very impressive. Each of us climbed up on the arch and took pictures. What an amazing find!

By now it was getting late so we decided to return to our small camp. On the way back, we could look down and see our red tent far off in the distance. I realized our tent was located in a very precarious spot in the valley. The northern slope stood out as a shear wall of rock which did not look very stable. Thinking back to the Great Buffoon, I realized the mountain could come down and cover our little tent like squashing a fly. We took our chances anyway and spent another night in the tent.

The next morning, we decided to climb up to the top of the mountain at the end of the valley. It was going to be a long hike, but both of us were up to the challenge. We headed up the slope going East toward the top of the mountain. The sky was clear and looked like another beautiful day. About halfway up, we came to a small plateau which contained a crystal-clear lake and looked like something from a story book. I would expect Hobbits to live near this lake. The small creek we were gold mining in came out of this lake. There were still patches of snow and ice around the shaded edges of the lake which added to its beauty.

We continued up the mountain following what I assumed were sheep trails. After about four hours we reached the top of the mountain. At the top was a small plateau, almost a shelf of flat rock that we could walk along. Mary and I found a couple of rocks to sit on and look out across the Brooks Range. We had only been there about 15 minutes when we heard a helicopter flying in the area. We spotted him coming along to the northeast of us. We watched as the helicopter landed and shut down on a point about four miles from us. A guy got out and walked a little way from the helicopter and proceeded to take a leak. Both Mary and myself began to yell as loud as we could and the noise vibrated all over the mountains. The guy looked all around trying to figure out where we were. He never did see us and we got quite a kick out of the thoughts that must have been going through his head. He had to have been thinking he was the only one in the world for miles around, but someone, somewhere was watching him.

We were still up on top of the mountain when right behind us a small cloud began to form. It was only about 5 feet by 5 feet and we could actually put our hands into it and swirl them around. It was very cool and damp in that small cloud and I had never seen anything like that on a clear sunny day. As we stood there and watched, the cloud continued to grow and soon it began to block our way off the mountain. Mary and I decided we should head back to our camp. Since it was all downhill, it took us only half the time to get back. But by the time we got back to our camp, the cloud turned into more clouds and was threatening to rain. It not only started to rain, but the wind and thunder also started. We barely got back to the tent before the down pouring rain started. We had to bundle up in the tent as the storm raged outside. I was sure the tent, with us inside of it, would blow away. I told Mary that would be the last time I would play around with a small cloud as I was sure it was taking vengeance on us for messing with it at the top of the mountain.

The next morning was as bright and clear as the mornings before. Everything was wet and steam was rolling off the hills around us. If it had not been for the steam and fog, one would never realize how hard the storm had hit the night before. We hung everything out to dry and ate some breakfast. By about ten o'clock in the morning, we were ready to head back down to the cabin. We loaded up our packs and started back down the mountain. We thought we would make it back that day, but the time went by faster than we thought and we found ourselves short by several miles when evening came. We noticed a couple of bears off in the distance on our trip down and now we felt the distinct feeling that one of them was following us. We set up our tent on a little rise of caribou moss so we could see all around us. Of course, after dark that did not help any. We had a very restless night of sleep and when we got up the next morning and prepared to leave, I noticed fresh bear tracks all around our little camp. I never told Mary about the bear tracks; after all, the bear never ate us. We were able to make it back to the cabin by early afternoon. Somewhere along the way we had found a large single caribou antler. I carried it back to the cabin and mounted it right over the cabin door on the ridge pole. We had a great adventure and both realized how lucky we were to be in this part of the world.

19

EVERYDAY LIVING IN
THE WILDERNESS

I have explained about my adventures, the people and unusual events during this time of my life. But I have not described the times of just enjoying the wilderness and being part of a world so few of us ever spend time in. I found myself reflecting on so many deep and mysterious things so few people have time to reflect on in today's fast-paced world. I would sit at the table that looked out across the southern Ambler Valley and write letters to people where the words came deep out of my heart like nowhere else. There was not a day gone by where I ever felt bored or could complain I had nothing to do. Quite the contrary; time went by so fast that when Mary and I had to leave, because of all our obligations back in the real world, we both cried our eyes out because we were leaving this all behind. We were never sure we could return and as it turned out, that was mostly the case.

During the building phase of the cabin, the days were filled with the sound of the chainsaw, hammering of nails and carving of wood. We were so intent on staying alive that we had little time to reflect on what it was really like to be there. Still I would find time to take my two boys out into the woods and teach them about things to look for and things to look out for. Since both Fred and Michael had been in the airplane crash with us, (which actually seemed to be cool to them), they would play airplane crash with two sticks in each hand. They would imagine flying around the woods and crashing into trees, into the ground, the cabin or each other. I realized neither of them would follow in my footsteps of being in aviation. To this day, that is the case. They also liked to make forts all over the woods and picked out their special area using scraps of wood from the cabin and limbs from the woods and built, what was in their minds, a special place to hang out. They also liked the river and the rocks in the river. The river was so clear and many of the rocks were full of color. Red from iron, green from copper and gray from the granite. They would find them along the river and put them into piles about one and half feet high. The piles would stay like a monument of time. When I went back to the cabin years later, the rock piles were still there.

I brought fishing tackle and poles with me when we came to the cabin. When we arrived, the river was iced over. As the ice melted, it formed large crystals about 6-8 inches long and about one inch across, with several sides, they looked like the Superman crystals in the Fortress of Solitude. We could hold them up to the light and have a prism effect all around. The boys loved those crystals. Of course, they didn't last long out of the river. Once the ice left the river, the fishing began. I took the kids out with me to the rock outcropping which went out into the river right near the cabin. It wasn't long before they both caught their first fish. They caught four large Arctic Grayling. There they stood with the fish on a stick holding them between the two of them, each with huge smiles on their faces. To this day, they both love to fish. After that successful day of fishing, they would drag me away from working on the cabin so they could catch more fish. Every evening and some mornings, we could be found along the Ambler River with our lines in the water.

One day before the ice had gone off the river, while we were all eating breakfast, we noticed a large herd of caribou walking up the gravel bar out front. As we watched them, they came to the edge of the river. At the front of the herd were about six large bulls with huge racks on their heads. They were without doubt the leaders of the herd. They surveyed the river ice and picked a route across the river and started walking across the ice. They made it across without a problem. The smaller bulls who were behind them, along with the rest of the herd, started milling around at the river's edge. Right at the spot where the large bulls had crossed was an opening in the ice. As we watched, suddenly the smaller bulls jumped into the river at the opening and swam under the ice. Without hesitation, the whole herd began to follow. We couldn't believe what we were seeing. It looked to us to be mass suicide. On the other side of the river was another opening in the ice. It did not look as large as the one they were entering, but they began coming up and through that hole on the other side of the river. As we watched, we could see that too many were trying to come up through the smaller hole on the other side. Many of the herd died trying to get out of the river. The whole time the older bulls stayed where they were on the other side of the river watching as most of their herd committed suicide. To this day I wonder what they were thinking, if anything at all. Just one of the many mysteries we saw in the valley.

Speaking of caribou, one day Mary and I were out on the gravel bar enjoying the warm sun. The mosquitoes were never as bad out on the gravel bar as they were in the woods; not as many things to suck blood from on the gravel bar. We were just strolling along minding our own business when out of nowhere came a lone caribou at a full run. This animal was in panic mode and didn't even slow down when it saw us. In fact, it almost ran right over us. That poor animal's eyes were as big as saucers and he wasn't letting anything get in its way. After he disappeared out into the woods, Mary looked at me and I looked at her and we both said at the same time "We need to go back to the cabin right now!" Whatever was chasing the caribou did not need to start chasing us. Whatever it was we never found out. One more mystery of the valley.

I haven't mentioned much about mosquitoes, but they were there in numbers. At times, it would get really annoying. I am not one to put on mosquito repellent, but for everyone else, it was a daily event; we called it our Alaska perfume. During the evening the mosquitoes were always worse and as the sun would get low on the horizon, the mosquitoes would come out in full force. Fortunately, I brought enough mosquito netting with me to cover the windows that we would open during the day. We also had Pic mosquito coils that we could use in the cabin when the mosquitoes snuck in. While I was gone picking up the airplane, Mary spent her spare time with the kids and she chinked the cabin walls with moss. She did such a good job that few mosquitoes got in except through the door when it was open. In the evening, I would take a pair of scissors and cut off the noses of the mosquitoes when they poked them through the screen. You never got bored at the cabin.... always something to do.

Once we had most of the work done at the cabin, we were able to enjoy our surroundings a little more. When one first begins living out in the remote woods, it can be a little intimidating and you can become fearful. There is an adjustment period, kind of like moving into a new neighborhood. The difference here was the fact that some of the neighbors wanted to eat you! It took us about thirty days to get used to our neighborhood, then the bears came out of hibernation and it took another few days to get used to what was going on in the near vicinity. Some mornings it would just be caribou, some mornings it would be a moose and other mornings a bear. We got used to certain bears being around so when a strange bear appeared, we were quick to get back into the cabin. Usually it was just a small black bear but occasionally it would be a grizzly bear. The grizzly bears never bothered us and usually they were just passing through. Still, when we were hiking out in the woods, we wore our bells and carried our gun. I mentioned before, the old joke was if you saw bear scat with bells in it while out in the woods, it most likely was a grizzly bear. Fortunately, we never found any bells but we did see a lot of bear scat.

Living in a cabin so far from civilization could be challenging at times. After all, we had no TV and cell phones hadn't been invented yet. We did have music, eight track tapes and a small generator. On the trip where I crashed the airplane I brought back a stereo radio with an eight-track tape player built in. Mary and I would crank up the music pretty loud some evenings and blast the sound down the valley. I always expected to see animals dancing across the gravel bar. I also had the CB radio and a long wire antenna stretched out across several trees with the wire coming back into the cabin. We were always surprised what we could hear late at night on the radio. Some nights we would pick up Russia and listen to propaganda that neither of us understood. One night we picked up a station out of Europe that was all music and news. During the time we were at the cabin, Jimmy Carter was President. Most the news was about peace talks and threatening war in the Middle East. In the Brooks Range, we cared little about the bad news.

In our supplies, I brought several 10 pound bags of flour. We also had lentils, powdered eggs, powdered milk, canned butter, canned meats and even canned bacon. We had salt and pepper as well as some other seasonings and I also had yeast to make bread, along with honey, cheese, peanut butter, jam and crackers.

With the granny oven, we could bake bread. It took several loaves to get the system down. The oven had to be around 400 degrees to start off with and stay there for about 15-20 minutes. Then the oven had to cool down to 350 degrees to finish cooking the bread. I finally figured out how to do it. The black spruce have real dry tops, or a cluster of branches, that Mary and I called flower tops. When we needed to make bread, we would gather a few flower tops, load the stove with them and then add regular wood behind that. The stove would light off and burn hot for about 15 minutes and then, just like that, cool down to 350 degrees. This made the most beautiful bread and would come out almost perfect every time. We even got good at making cinnamon rolls. Sometimes we would roll our fish in batter that we made and deep fry them in cooking oil -- so good!

We had a large wash tub. Not one of those round wash tubs, but a large oval tub style. We could actually get our whole body into the wash tub and the kids could almost swim in it. We used the wash tub to take baths in as well as do our laundry. We brought laundry soap, regular soap and dish soap. We usually took baths once a week unless we got dirtier during the week. It was almost a full day project for us as we would heat up water on the stove and add cold water from the river to make enough water to bathe or do laundry. We did our laundry down by the river so we could rinse out the soap and we would hang our wet clothes all around the stove to dry. It was quite a sight to see. The kids hated bath day as they liked playing in the woods more than anything else.

In the cabin, we had the covered drain board with a wash tub to do dishes in. We even had a homemade dish rack to dry the dishes on and we also had a three-gallon tea pot that never left the stove. We always kept water in the pot so it was hot when we needed it. I built a four-foot by four-foot table that set in front of the window so you could look down the valley. We spent a lot of time at the table writing letters and reading books and we used it as our breakfast and dinner table. I covered the wood table top with clear Visqueen and stapled it down to the underside which made it easy to clean.

During the middle of summer, we enjoyed 24 hours of daylight. But by the time August and September rolled around, it was getting dark at night and earlier each day. I built candle holders from beer cans and placed them around the cabin in specific spots. We had two candles over the bed for our reading lights. I brought the small generator so I could run the radios or a 100-watt light bulb. We didn't use the generator much, but when we needed to, we had it to use. Overall, living in the cabin was a pretty good life.

In the fall, the forest was abundant with mushrooms and blueberries. We could get up in the morning take a coffee cup out in the yard and pick enough blue berries to make a great stack of pancakes. We even had syrup for the pancakes, but if we had time, we would make syrup out of the blueberries. We found out from our neighbors up river which mushrooms were good to eat. We spent a few evenings out looking for our favorite kind which had a taste similar to chicken. We called them chicken delights. They really spruced up a meal in the evening and they also went great in powdered eggs.

The land around the cabin provided us with fish, berries and mushrooms. If I wanted, the area would have provided us with moose meat, caribou meat, ducks, geese and spruce hens. But we were not spending the winter there, so building up a lot in food supplies would not have been a good idea.

We were always out cutting firewood which was plentiful and all over the place so it was just a matter of taking the chainsaw out and finding dead trees. The hard part was hauling the wood back to the cabin. Over the spring and summer, we gathered quite a lot of fire wood. We always had some sort of project going on which kept me busy most of the time. The first big project outside the cabin was the outhouse. That took a few days to build. It required a small building with a roof that didn't leak and a small bench to put the seat on. I put a screen door on the outhouse mostly because of the mosquitoes. It wasn't much to look at, but with the toilet seat on the bench and the deep hole we dug, it did the job and the best part was the view. The outhouse set on the edge of the river bank about 75 feet away from the cabin looking down the valley toward the Bornite mine. No matter how bad one needed to go, you always did a bear check before heading to the outhouse.

During the month that I was fixing the airplane, I decided the cabin needed a high cache. I had time while waiting for parts in between repairs. The fun part about building in the woods on your own homestead is the freedom to design and do what you want. I was alone in the woods without either the kids or Mary around for the whole month of August. Near the cabin was a large white spruce tree. The bark beetles had gotten to it, the tree was almost dead and it was so close to the cabin that critters could jump from the tree to the roof of the cabin with ease. I decided to make the tree the base for my high cache. I first made a very long ladder, used the ladder to clear all the limbs off the tree as high as I could reach. Then I built a platform around the tree as far up as I could safely go. Once I got the structure secured to the tree, I cut boards and covered the structure making a floor. I put a trap door in the floor so I could put steps on the tree leading up to the door. Once the platform was finished I built another platform on top of that which was about eight feet above the lower platform. The second platform was smaller in size. I put another trap door in the floor with steps nailed to the tree going from the lower platform to the upper platform trap door. Once everything was secure, I climbed on the upper platform and left about six feet of tree sticking up and I cut off the rest of the top of the tree. Then I attached four poles, one at each corner of the two platforms, tying them together. Once this was all done, I wrapped the four sides in black Griffolyn and secured the Griffolyn with cap strips over the poles. When I finished the high cache, it was an awesome site and stood up above the cabin by several feet where the view from the top platform was amazing. I knew the wind would blow it over if I didn't tie it off. I had some very large rope with me and used the rope to tie off the very top of the tree to both ends of the ridge pole of the cabin and used one rope down to the ground at the base of another tree. This gave the high cache a tripod-like strength. The last thing I did was wrap about four feet of the bottom of the tree with stainless steel sheet metal like what I used on the countertop inside the cabin. The stainless steel kept the animals from climbing the tree. Not even a squirrel could get up to the new high cache. People coming up the valley would always see the high cache before noticing the cabin.

Once Mary returned and saw what I had built in her absence, she was a bit shocked. She wondered how I hadn't killed myself hanging off that tall tree. Looking at it from the ground, I wondered myself. It took some courage to climb up to the top platform. Mary finally went up with me to the top and she, like I, was amazed at the view from up there. We would go up there in the evenings and watch for animals coming up the valley. It was almost like a religious experience.

It may sound like the weather was always sunny and I wish that were so, but there were times when the clouds and rain would fill up the valley for days. When we needed good weather though, the rain clouds would part and the sun would return. Still there were times when we would spend days huddled around the wood stove keeping dry as it stormed outside. Those days were particularly hard on the kids because they loved to be outside playing around the cabin or down near the creek. I am sure it drove Mary and me a little crazy when the rain lasted too long, but it does not seem to be a part I remember. Perhaps it could be selective memory or it really wasn't as bad as we thought at the time. I do remember, however, one specific storm that literally blew in with a vengeance. The wind blew very hard and the rain came in spurts at a sideways slant. Just going out to get the firewood that day was a challenge. The trees were whipping around and I was sure a few would blow over. The outhouse did blow over, but that was easy to stand back up. The weather in the valley was not always perfect.

20

TIME TO GO

I had to stay at the cabin for five months in the fifth year to prove up on the homestead. The week following our arrival at the cabin in April, the BLM flew over with a small plane, I believe to check on whether or not we had made it to the property and cabin in time. During the middle of the summer we were surprised by a visit from the BLM. There were two guys who had come down the river. They floated down the Ambler River by canoe and were visiting all the cabins along the way. They got to our cabin late in the afternoon, so we invited them in for dinner and offered a place to stay for the night. Mary had just come back from Fairbanks and her trip down to Minnesota. She brought wine and fresh vegetables upon her return. They were shocked when we put on a four-course meal and finished it off with a fine bottle of wine. They really enjoyed their stay with us. I put the extensions on the kids bunk beds and they spent the night in comfort instead of in a tent out on the ground. The next day they had breakfast with us, (blueberry pancakes and eggs) and then said a very friendly goodbye to us and floated off down the river toward the Village of Ambler.

Toward the end of the five months, a BLM representative landed a plane out on the gravel bar and came over and talked with us. It was very near the last week of the five months. We fed him dinner and spent some time talking with him and turned out to be a great visit for Mary and me. He was very impressed with what we had accomplished in the short few months we had been there. He realized we had really made it a home. With all the inspections and visits, I knew I had passed all the requirements to keep the homestead. About four years later I received the official Patent on the land and can say it truly is my homestead.

Of course, all good things must come to an end. As September ended and October began, the temperatures began to drop. We would wake up in the morning and have flashbacks on how cold we had been the first few weeks we had spent at the cabin. I would climb out of bed, get my clothes on, head for the wood pile, get the fire going and warm up the cabin.

We set the date for leaving to be October 3rd. As that date approached, we both began to feel somewhat sad. It had been a lifetime adventure that in so many ways changed both of our lives forever. There were so many hardships we had overcome. We had seen things that few people will ever see. Some were only for us and some would never be seen again. Mary and I had a new appreciation for who we were and what we could accomplish. I became a better pilot and I was no longer afraid of the gravel bar. Mary was a strong individual when I first met her, but she had a very soft and sensitive side to her that I found while we spent our time together out in the woods. She left the cabin a very positive person with a much better idea of who and what she wanted to be.

I also realized why people stayed together so many years ago. People relied on each other to survive in a world which could kill you in a heartbeat. Today the world is a land of plenty and we throw things away just because we get tired of them. We forget the importance of feeling alive and sharing it with someone with whom you care for and they care for you. Life on this planet is very hard, but as Mary and I learned out in the wilderness, it's not the planet that is hard, it is us who make it so hard. Every day we woke up in the cabin was exciting. We had no idea what to expect or what would happen on any given day. We had no control of our destiny and we loved the challenge and the opportunity. Maybe that is the secret of life...to just let go of all expectations and what little control we think we have, and let the days happen with no expectations; let God guide you as He sees fit.

One morning, it was October 3rd and the adventure at the cabin was over. We took only our personal items and our memories. The plane was going to be loaded to the max with full tanks of fuel and the two of us. I knew, as I looked at our load, that getting off the gravel bar was going to be close. With tears in our eyes we both said goodbye to this little piece of what we felt was paradise. Promises were made that we would be back someday and yet we knew it could never be the same. We made the decision to leave, though in our hearts, we really wanted to stay. Life back with my kids and at my company were demanding my return.

Mary got in the cockpit of the airplane and held the brakes while I pulled the propeller through. The plane started on the first pull. I got into the pilot's side of the airplane and checked all five of the gauges. I pushed forward on the throttle and held my brakes till the RPM was up to speed. I let off the brakes and held the plane on the ground until just before we hit the water with the wheels. I pulled back on the wheel and the plane lifted off and into the air. I made one more pass over the cabin and then we were gone.

The flight back to Circle City went without any problems. We landed in Circle City and everyone came out to welcome us home. Then Mary and I took the airplane to Fairbanks where I picked up the kids and I drove my truck back to Circle City. I left the plane in Fairbanks until I had the opportunity to drive back and pick it up.

Mary stayed with me through the winter of 1978-1979. She taught school in Circle City while I worked on the helicopters. In the spring, she went back to Minnesota to finish school and her degree. We drifted apart and went on to start new lives.

During the next summer, Sunshine Helicopters ran into some financial difficulties and I was forced to sell my airplane. The company went on for several more years, but I was unable to purchase another airplane. Without having the airplane, I had to rely on caching rides with other people to get up to the cabin. My life became very busy raising two boys and working in the aviation industry.

I eventually moved back to Oregon where I lived and raised Fred and Michael. I would still return to Alaska each summer and work out in the field on the helicopters. Many of these trips included the boys going with me. They were able to travel and see Alaska like few kids ever get to do. Fred still lives in Alaska, and I believe Michael will return again someday. I am now going on 28 years since I moved back to Alaska full time. There is a freedom here in this amazing state that I can find nowhere else.

In 1983, Gordon was killed when a building collapsed on him in Circle City. I had already sold out of the company by then, but losing Gordon was a very sad day for all of us and the true Alaskan that he was, made it a loss for the whole state. His wife eventually sold out of Circle City and turned in the Sunshine Helicopter certificate back to the FAA. If you want to fly on a Sunshine Helicopter, you can do so in Hawaii.

Many years have now gone by and I am sure many wonder why I never returned to live at the cabin. I guess it was a magical time in my life and to try to duplicate that time would be impossible. By now, none of the people who lived up there then are anywhere to be found. Mary moved away to Arizona and has found a happy life for herself, yet I know the mysteries of that year will always be special for her like they have been for me.

21

RETURN TO THE CABIN

I flew back to the cabin in a helicopter a few years later. I spent one week there with my golden retriever, Ginger. When we landed, Ginger ran around sniffing the ground and the area surrounding the cabin. The hair stood up on her back the whole time. After I offloaded the supplies from the helicopter, the pilot was getting ready to leave. Ginger made a dash for the helicopter and to this day, I can still see her with her paws on the cargo rack begging to get inside and leave the area. As the helicopter lifted off the ground and she could no longer reach the cargo rack, she dashed back to me and buried her whole body between my legs. She looked up at me like I was crazy for staying behind. She definitely sensed something about the area which I was unaware of, but I would soon find out.

I remember opening the cabin door a huge wave of nostalgia washed over me. The cabin was exactly like we had left it several years prior. No dust on the counter and no dust on the table. The calendar was still on October 1978. Pots and pans were still on the drain board where we had put them to dry the morning we left. The writing table with notes and unfinished letters were setting there untouched. I cannot begin to explain the feelings that washed over me those first few minutes.

The only damage to the cabin came from a marten who had moved in and tore up the foam bedding. I chased him out and closed up the hole. The next morning, I was awakened by the cabin shaking and the roof moving. I thought at first it was the marten knocking things around in the cabin. The cabin shook again and I thought "that has to be the biggest marten in the world!" I jumped out of bed and noticed Ginger was buried under the bed and not at all eager to come. The cabin shook again and that's when I noticed the West facing window was covered in brown hair. As I watched, I realized it was a large grizzly bear outside the cabin lifting the edge of the roof with his paws. I grabbed my gun and went out the front door and very carefully looked around the corner of the cabin. The bear was standing on his hind legs looking at me. I could tell he was puzzled by my presence and I think he was wondering where I had come from. It was like he had been there at the cabin several times before but no one was there. I yelled at him to go away, but he just stood there looking at me. I shot a round over his head and he got back down on his four feet, turned and walked into the woods. He was not in any hurry. This was my "welcome back" bear. I must admit, Ginger stayed very close to my side the rest of the time we were there.

Ginger and I stayed only one week. The helicopter came back to pick us up because the company had an emergency and needed me back sooner than I wanted to leave.

■ ■ ■

Alaska is His place
There is something there
To which his heart returns
A vibrancy, a don't-give a damn,
Holler-at-the-bears-feeling!!!
Written By: Victoria B. Domke

Made in the
USA
Middletown, DE